SHED OR
YOU'RE DEAD®

---

31 Unconventional Strategies
for Growth & Change

KATHY B. DEMPSEY

Trey Press
Phoenix, Arizona

Shed or You're Dead®:
31 Unconventional Strategies for Growth and Change

Kathy B. Dempsey

Published by:
Trey Press
Phoenix, Arizona

Photography by: Jeff Green
Artwork by: Joe Kulka

Printed in the United States of America

ISBN: 097429262-1

PRAISE FOR SHED OR YOU'RE DEAD®: 31 UNCONVENTIONAL STRATEGIES FOR GROWTH AND CHANGE

"*Shed or You're Dead®* — Buy it and see if you're up to Kathy Dempsey's exciting challenge. Her book of unconventional change strategies contains work well worth doing!"

Chris Clarke-Epstein, CSP
Consultant and Author, *78 Important Questions Every Leader Needs to Ask and Answer*

"*31 Unconventional Strategies for Growth and Change* is a powerful catalyst for corporate, association, personal change and growth! Kathy Dempsey challenges the identification and strategies necessary for moving from success to significance."

Naomi Rhode, CSP, CPAE Speaker Hall of Fame
Past President National Speakers Association
Co-Founder Smart Practice

"Any one of us who has been blessed to know Kathy Dempsey knows first-hand the incredible force for reflection, examination and change that Kathy and Lenny represent! Now that energy and insight is available to all! Buy this book and share it!"

Sam Waltz, former CEO & Board Chairman,
Public Relations Society of America (PRSA)

"It's quick, it's fun, but most importantly it's useful! Kathy Dempsey gives some easy to use strategies that will make you stop and think. This book could make a real difference in your life."

Jennie Doremus, SPHR, Vice President of
Human Resources, US Xpress Enterprises

"Special people DO come into our lives for important reasons— Kathy Dempsey and Lenny have been gracious enough to share a portion of their great wisdom with me. Now the world can learn the secret to shedding straight from the lizard's mouth!"

Gail Pollock, Executive Director,
Habitat for Humanity of Chattanooga

"Kathy Dempsey's *Shed or You're Dead®: 31 Unconventional Strategies for Growth and Change*, is an inspiring devotional to yourself!"

John Reddish, Managing Director,
Advent Management International

"The introspection that accompanied Kathy's own personal growth experience has given her keen powers of observation about the important lessons to be learned on life's journey."

Pat Cahill, Former CEO,
Catholic Health Initiatives

"Kathy and Lenny make it crystal clear in their easy 31 unconventional strategies how to shed for change and growth. They give us the strategies—all we need to do is pick one and start shedding."

Carol A. Kivler, President,
Kivler Communications

DEDICATION

To my awesome nephew Trey Abbott who,
along with his lizard Razor, continually reminds me
to shed and enjoy the journey!

TABLE OF CONTENTS

ACKNOWLEDGMENTS

I would like to acknowledge some incredible blessings in my life. I have had the privilege of having two extremely supportive parents. Katie Bleuer, my mom, who died of cancer in 1992 and Ernie Bleuer, my father, who tragically died due to a car accident in 2000.

Virginia Carraher (a.k.a. Sister Virginia Elephant), my sister, who had to put up with years of "loving sibling torture" from her older sister. (Sorry Gin, I still feel bad about the pepper biscuit!) and to my beloved brother-in-law Michael, who I still haven't forgiven for dyeing my cat, Alex, red!

Mom said some special people would come into my life. Here they are...

JoAnn Alexander, one of the best leaders and human beings I have ever had the privilege of knowing. Her belief in me allowed the nurturing elements that were necessary to fertilize my soil. Under those conditions I could do nothing else but blossom, follow my passion, and start my own business as a professional speaker, consultant and author. JoAnn continues to challenge me to be much more than I could ever dream of being.

Some incredible mentors: Bob Pike, Naomi Rhode, Elizabeth Jeffries, Zig Ziglar, Betsy Allen, John Bolinger, Margaret Trimpey, Austin McGonigle, and Pat Cahill. All incredible mentors who have shared their knowledge, expertise, and offered support.

I would have never made it through some huge periods of

shedding had it not been for some dear friends who have, each in their own way, offered incredible support exactly when I needed it. Shirley Garrett, June Cline, Patty Kitching, Marcia Steele, Steve Cohn, Edie Rimas, Ronnie Johnson, Bobbie Ingram, Betsy Chapin Taylor, Jim Smith Jr., Bill Wilson, LaVerne Dempsey, Rick Horsey, Phil Summerlin, Ann Laymon, Phyllis Maynor, Sam Horn, Bob Danzig, Andrea Pike, Susan Jensen, Sister Judy Raley, David Ryback, David Mann, Pat Harmon, Carol Kivler, Heshie Segal, John Reddish, Chris Silcox, Fred Melton, Cliff Smith, Grace Brame, and Barry Kardos.

And to Dyerenda Johnson, one of my best friends, who was in a tragic car accident in May 2003. No matter what my state of mind, Dyerenda always made me laugh. She loved life and people. She always lit up a room with her presence. Her laugh will live on with the thousands of hearts that she touched.

A special thanks to Sam Waltz. I will never forget how you helped me sketch out my initial ideas for this book on the back of an envelope.

And my utmost gratitude goes to Chris Clarke-Epstein who has been my guide, support, and slave master! If it wasn't for her you wouldn't be reading this book. And to her daughter, Miriam Phillips, who continues to share words of wisdom, not to mention that she's adopted Lenny and me into the family!

FOREWORD

G reetings from the Lizard World!

I believe you are about to experience one of the strangest, yet most insightful books you will every read. At least it was for me. Being a top graduate of Reptile University, I am very well read. But this is actually the first human book that has captured my attention and helped me shed in ways I would never have dreamed.

Let me share with you what I experienced after I read this book.

- My heart was touched, my thinking was challenged.
- I experienced a variety of emotions (happy, sad, inspired, intrigued)!
- I learned two to three strategies that I could immediately implement to help me deal with change, accelerate my growth, and shed my skin!

My gecko guess is that you will too!

Kathy and I first met several years ago in Chattanooga, Tennessee. She had approached me about working together. We had some conversations about what that might look like. But before I agreed to be her life-long business partner, I ordered a comprehensive background check from the HBI (Human Bureau of Investigation). Let me share with you what the HBI found:

Kathy was born in Washington, DC (George Washington University Hospital, fifth floor to be exact). Her parents moved her as a teenager (against her will) to Chattanooga, Tennessee. Being the bright, young, mature woman that she was at age 14, she focused her efforts on developing her mission in life—to make her parents' life hell. Investigators reported she had even left nasty messages under her parents' pillows like, "take me back to DC or else!"

When her rebellious tactics did not work, she settled down and began her career as an ER nurse. Later she earned an M.Ed. in psychology from The University of Tennessee. She was also Administrator of Psychiatric/Alcohol and Drug Abuse Services and Educational Services for Memorial Healthcare System for many years and led their organizational development efforts.

I also found out some other interesting facts about Kathy:

- Honored for leading the strategic organizational development efforts of one of the **Top 100 Hospitals in America**.

- **Past President**, National Speakers Association, Philadelphia Chapter.

- Voted **Showcase Speaker of the Year** for the Georgia Speakers Association (GSA).

- Founder of **The Keep Shedding Educational Foundation** 501(c)(3) which sends African AIDS orphans to school.

- Achieved the highest earned speaker's designation in the world, **the Certified Speaking Professional (CSP)**.

The report also attributed these words to describe her:

- Energetic
- Engaging
- Unconventional

- Deep sense of mission
- Thought-provoking insights
- Driven to deliver results!

The HBI's final conclusion? "Engage with Kathy—she is a wonderful human being, full of life, and has many insightful lessons to share with the human race. Only caution—beware, she has been seen in airports talking to a plastic lizard!" I have found this to be completely accurate!

She checked out and seemed like a pretty cool lady so...

I decided to start a company, Keep Shedding! Inc., with her. Kathy is the President (50-50 co-owner with me) and I am the CEO (Chief Energy Officer). Our mission is to ignite individuals and organizations with the skills and motivation to lead and master change. Kathy does the motivational speaking, training, and consulting and I provide the real wisdom behind the scene.

After years of pleading, Kathy finally agreed to relocate from the East Coast and move to Scottsdale, Arizona to be closer to my relatives. I have been traveling around the country with Kathy for thirteen years now. What an adventure! Lots of FUN! Never a dull moment!

Anyway, my wish is that you enjoy this book and shed your skin as much as I did.

Ready, Set, SHED!

Sincerely,

Lenny T. Lizard

Chief Energy Officer
Keep Shedding! Inc.

INTRODUCTION

W hy read this book?

Since I was a child, I can always remember my mother, an elementary school teacher, asking one question everyday when I walked in the door, "Kathy, what did you learn in school today?"

Some days the lessons were more obvious and clear, like "If you talk too much, you will get sent to the principal's office." (I somehow seemed to be there a lot growing up...but you can see that I have channeled that "little problem" into a career as a successful professional speaker!)

What I have discovered over the years is that I learn more from the mistakes I make then the successes and I learn something from everyone I meet.

That is what *Shed or You're Dead®: 31 Unconventional Strategies for Growth and Change* is about. Learning from EVERYONE! Many people have been my teachers, most of them without even knowing it. A lot of them are people who, to most of us, would be considered extremely unhealthy and maladaptive. (But aren't we all a little neurotic?)

WARNING! Many of the thoughts and ideas in this book smack right in the face of conventional wisdom. Some of you will read sections of this book and say, "Kathy is crazy" (trust me, you will). But I would ask one thing. Stay with me and be open to what you can learn...even from the crazy strategies!

MY STORY: "KATHY, YOU'VE GOT . . ."

They told me I was going to die. My ears burned as Dr. Gazaleh blurted out, "Kathy, your AIDS test...it's come back positive!" That Wednesday afternoon in May of 1987 would never be forgotten.

As I hung up the phone, a tremor started through my hands, and then it accelerated through the rest of my body.

I was in shock. My worst nightmare had come true. I was a nurse working in the ER during June 1986 when an accident-related trauma patient was wheeled in. We had to crack open his chest to perform internal CPR. My hands had been wrist-deep inside him. But despite our best efforts, he died minutes later.

Later that night, we found out he had AIDS. My own heart skipped a beat as I looked down at my hands and remembered a minor cut on my right index finger. Believe it or not, but back in the mid-80's we didn't wear latex gloves to protect us.

Because of the exposure, the doctors decided to test me every three months for a year. After three negative tests, I thought I was home free. I was wrong!

After the dreadful call in May, I rushed to the hospital to meet with the doctors. My head was spinning. I couldn't think. My hands were shaking; I could barely grip the steering wheel.

This just couldn't be true. Why me? I was a nurse—trying to help a patient. I was not ready to die! I was just 26 years old.

The doctors decided to run additional tests to confirm the positive results. My nightmare continued. Two weeks later, the confirmatory tests also came back positive. The doctors notified the Centers for Disease Control (CDC), now also concerned.

You see, I was the first healthcare worker in America to test HIV-positive from an on-the-job exposure.

AIDS, just six years after it was discovered in May 1981, remained a guaranteed death sentence. Most AIDS victims did not survive more than a year. People feared AIDS they way they'd feared leprosy, maybe more. Speculation was rampant, but no one really knew all the ways it could be spread.

No, this can't happen to me, I angrily thought. *I can't handle it! What am I going to do? Not only am I HIV positive, but now it looks like I'm going to be a media spectacle—a poster child for the CDC.* It was more than I could bear.

Reluctantly, that night I sat down and told my family. A family of faith in a community that sometimes saw the disease as a curse, my Mom and Dad and sister Virginia were supportive.

Then, after mentally laboring for days, I forced myself to tell my boss. Dr. McGuire was sympathetic, but said, "Kathy, if this gets out, this hospital will shut down. I'm sorry, but you can't work here anymore."

That weekend, I shared the shocking news with my church. To my amazement, some members turned away from me. They viewed AIDS as God's punishment on the gay community! That I was not gay and that I had contracted HIV by trying to help someone seemed to escape their attention. Even some of my friends became distant. I guess they were afraid of catching the disease from me.

I stopped eating. I stopped sleeping. One night in a graduate school class, as I wrestled with my own demons, my professor announced a film, *Living With AIDS*. Sitting in the classroom, chest tight and head spinning, I watched young people at the prime of their lives waste away in hospitals. My classmates talked in horror of the disease. Little did they know who was sitting beside them.

That night I determined one thing: I was not going to die the slow, agonizing death of an AIDS victim. I was not going to waste away. I could not! I would not! I decided I would choose how I would die.

After class, I started driving, until I found myself in the parking lot of Chattanooga's most famous hotel.

My mind started racing. It raced for hours around a track called "regrets." Regrets of not spending more time with my family and friends. I was always too busy, too stressed. Regrets of not taking the time to find out who Kathy Dempsey was.

All alone, I sat in my car that dark, drizzling night with a bottle of sleeping pills in my hand. I was a nurse. I knew what it took...

I was jolted back into reality by three knocks on my car window. It was Robin, one of my friends, from out of nowhere. "Kathy, are you OK?" she asked.

With tears streaming down my face, I despairingly shook my head, "No. I am scared and lonely." Robin climbed into the car beside me. We talked. We cried. It went on for hours.

But now, with Robin's intervention, caring and support, I found I had the strength inside me that I needed to go forward. From her, and from others whose love and support I'd forgotten, I found my hope, as well!

But, the story doesn't end there.

Three months after my initial test, I received another phone call from Dr. Gazelah. "Kathy, I am not sure how to tell you this...but your tests, all eight of your tests, have come back negative. The CDC says you don't have AIDS!"

As I hung up the phone, I felt like a thousand-pound weight had been lifted from my chest.

Some people call it a medical error; I call it a miracle. What a gift! I had thought my life was over...and now I had it back. It was like a VCR and I got to push "rewind."

All those regrets, now I could do something about them. I thanked God and promised myself from that day forward, "I will not live my life the same way again."

So, you ask, "Kathy, what did you do differently after your AIDS scare?"

Well, I woke up. Insanely, I had been sleeping for 26 years. This was the wake up call of my life. Now, it was my choice whether I was going to hit the snooze button or not. Not everyone gets a second chance; I thought I'd better take advantage of it.

That personal trauma, I found, was indeed a blessing. From that moment forward, I was committed to the task of remaking my life, to finding ways to create the legacy that I wanted to leave, that is, to leave the world a better place for my having been a part of it.

From that moment forward, I made a conscious decision to SHED.

WHAT IS SHEDDING?

The Philosophy of Shedding

Let me introduce you to what has become my personal philosophy of life by sharing my journal entry dated July 29, 1998.

It was 7 a.m. Time for our quarterly Ethics meeting at the hospital. As I rushed into the room at the last minute, I ran into a guy, David Mann, I hadn't seen in a while. "Good morning David and how are you?"

"I am fine, Kathy...but my lizard is dead."

Startled yet intrigued, I asked "Your lizard is dead! What happened?"

"He didn't shed his skin...and if lizards don't shed their skin, they die."

"Why?" I asked.

He explained. "Lizards grow by shedding their skin. If they don't shed their skin, they aren't growing. Lizards die if they don't grow."

After I thought for a moment, I said, "David, what can we learn from the lizard?"

With a perplexed look on his face, he replied. "We all need to grow, we need to grow physically, mentally, spiritually...and how we grow is to shed our old skin. If we don't grow as humans, we'll die."

"And David, what does our old skin represent? Maybe old habits, negative thoughts, unhealthy relationships?"

Simultaneously, we looked at each other...the light bulb had gone on. "Shed or you're dead!"

Two things had happened that day. First, it gave me a benchmark for my personal growth path. Second, because David had been placed on my path that day, I had a metaphor – "Shed or You're Dead," featuring Lenny the Lizard, who soon would become my life's companion and personal vehicle for helping others.

It grieves me to know that my parents are not alive to see this book become a reality. My mother, right before she died, shared with me how sad she was that she could not be around to see me continue to grow and develop. She told me that God was going to send some incredible people along my way to help me on my journey. "Look for them..." she instructed me.

Little did my mother realize that one of them would be a lizard named Lenny.

Shedding is growing, Lenny tells people, because on one side it is letting go of the old, on the other side, it's gaining of the new.

What Causes Us to Shed?

What causes us to shed?

Change!

Change is an inevitable phenomenon, a given, a fact of life. Indeed it is part of life.

And yet most of us, in varying degrees, fear change. Why? Because it's painful!

William Bridges, in his book *Transitions*, talks about change being comprised of three stages. Endings, transitions and new beginnings. He suggests that the endings and beginnings are not the difficult part, it is the transition between.

Shedding, or what Bridges calls the transition stage, is the painful process of letting go of the old and moving on to the new.

We live in a world that is rapidly accelerating, a world demanding a little more each day than the day before; a world where change seems like our only constant.

Did you know?

- World knowledge is doubling every 18 months.

- The average person makes 1,500 decisions a day vs. 25 just 100 years ago.

- The divorce rate has quadrupled over the past 30 years.

- In 1900, U.S. agriculture was 50% of the economy and job force, now it represents 1%.

- One in four people will develop cancer sometime in their life.

Whether it's a death, birth, divorce, marriage, loss of job, new job, broken relationship, new love, financial hardship, financial gain, getting sick, or getting well, it's all about change…it's all about shedding.

Life is all about change. Change is all about shedding. Shedding is all about letting go of the loss in order to gain something new. And just like the lizard we must shed.

"Change is hard because people overestimate the value of what they have—and underestimate the value of what they may gain by giving that up."
James Belasco, Author

What's at the Core of Change?

What's at the core of change? LOSS

When you look at change, you can't help but look at loss. For at the very essence of change is loss. With every change, a loss of some kind occurs.

Think of some changes that have occurred to you over the past few years. Job, illness, marriage, divorce, or a move. What were the losses? I would venture to say that the changes all encompassed a variety of losses, even if it was just the loss of the status quo.

So with change comes loss and with loss comes grief.

CHANGE = LOSS   LOSS = GRIEF

What is grief? It is a normal response to a loss.

The genesis of grief begins with the twin necessities of attachment and detachment. Do you remember being born?

26

Probably not, but just take a minute and imagine it. Just imagine being in your mother's womb. Think about what you might have said.

"Ahhh...It's so warm and secure in here. I don't have a worry in the world! All my needs are taken care of. I have no bills to pay, no kids to feed, no bosses to please. This is the life!"

Okay, enjoy living in your blissful amniotic-fluid world while it lasts! Because all of the sudden, 9 months later, reality strikes and wham bang, you are traumatically jolted from your serene surroundings and forced out into a cold, cruel world.

Quickly, the doctor grabs his scissors and cuts your cord. And what did you do? Well, I would guess that you screamed bloody murder!

Why? Because you were physically attached to your mother and someone "detached" you!

May I submit to you that this was your first loss? Your first shedding experience.

From the time you were born to the time you will die you will continuously experience a series of losses. You will experience attachments/detachments over and over again. The attachments and detachments won't be like the physical one that you experienced when the doctor cut your cord but life will continue to be a series of emotional attachments and detachments.

Now, if you had to deal with something continuously from birth to death, doesn't it make sense to know how to deal with it? But where do we learn? Did you take a Change 101 course in high school? Most of us didn't.

So where did we learn how to deal with it? We watched others, our parents, teachers, and friends who may or may not have had the healthiest responses.

27

Healthy shedding depends on your ability to navigate through life's attachments and detachments. Healthy shedding transforms change into gain and excitement into energy.

CHANGE = GAIN   EXCITEMENT = ENERGY

Lenny's Five Laws of Shedding

1. Shedding is a natural part of growth.
2. Shedding is about loss and gain.
3. Shedding offers us the greatest opportunity for growth.
4. Shedding is a choice.
5. Shedding is nurtured within a support environment.

Lenny's Challenge: Take 60 seconds, and ask yourself, "Which one of these laws is the most significant to me?"

_____

_____

_____

_____

Why?

_____

_____

_____

What Are the Results You Want?

What do you want to look like in your new skin?

A minister friend recently shared with me a story of a prominent religious leader.

After many years of faithful service, one day Reverend Glass died. As you might expect, he gracefully landed at the pearly gates. And who do you think he was greeted by? Saint Peter, of course.

"Hello Saint Peter. I am ready to come in," Reverend Glass enthusiastically exclaimed.

"Good to see you, Reverend Glass. Let me just go and double check the list," Saint Peter replied as he turned through The Big Book.

After a quick glance, St. Peter smiled and said, "Of course you are on the list, come on in Reverend Glass," and he handed the Rev. a wooden staff and cotton robe.

Reverend Glass strutted right into heaven.

Well, minutes later, a New York taxi cab driver also died. To everyone's surprise, he ended up at the pearly gates as well.

"Hey Pete, How's 'bout opening those gates man, I am ready to come on in and see whatsa happen'n."

Saint Peter shook his head as he repulsively looked down at his holey jeans, tattered shirt, and nasty unkept beard and said, "I don't know...let me go and check the list."

As he turned through the Big Book, his face froze. "Wow, he is on the list!" St. Peter perked up and congratulated the taxi cab driver.

"Come on in," he gleefully welcomed him and handing him a golden staff and a pearly robe.

Well, who do you think overheard the conversation? Reverend Glass. He stomped back up to Saint Peter and blurted out, "What is the deal? I am the world renowned Reverend Glass, I get a wooden staff and a cotton robe and this pathetic taxi cab driver gets a golden staff and a pearly robe? Why? Please tell me why?"

Saint Peter said, "It's simple. Results!"

"When you preached, people slept. When he drove, people prayed!"

Results. When all is said and done, results matter. You can have the best of intentions in life, but unless you get the results and outcomes that you want, what does it matter? How do you get the outcomes you want? You must stop and think about them now.

Here are some questions that may be helpful to answer:

- Who am I?
- What am I passionate about?
- What creates energy for me?
- What fuels my soul?
- What would I do if I didn't have to make money to live?
- What do I want to be saying on my 80th birthday about my life?
- What are my goals?

For me, I didn't have a clue about the answers to the most basic questions in life. Who am I? I was so busy, so wrapped up in my hectic world that I had never stopped long enough to answer that significant question.

Finally, it took a crisis to wake me up. It took sitting in my car contemplating suicide, the lowest point in my life, to make me realize that one of my regrets was that I never had taken the time to find out who Kathy Dempsey was.

After my AIDS crisis, I decided to begin my search and delve deeper into answering that question. My first step was to get counseling. Another was attending a silent spiritual retreat in Switzerland, where the focus was to answer one question. Who am I?

Walking into the retreat I answered that question by saying I was a sister, an administrator, a daughter, a friend. By the end of the retreat, that original answer was the farthest from the truth.

What I discovered was that all those were just roles that I was playing. And if we define ourselves by roles, then when those roles change or go away, through events such as death, divorce or loss of job, that can often lead to an identity crises.

The blessing of the retreat, for me, was discovering that who I am is a gift of God and that I am a spiritual being on a human journey for a few years.

What is my passion? For several years I struggled with that question. I had no clue! Finally, I decided to make answering that question my goal by journaling everyday. At the time, I was working as the administrator for psychiatric, alcohol and drug abuse services at the hospital. One day, I received a phone call asking me to begin speaking in the community on stress management. With some hesitation, I agreed. I hung up the phone and thought to myself, "They have definitely chosen the right person to teach these classes. I am the most stressed out person in this town!"

Several months later I was reading over my journal entries and I could see a developing trend. Week after week I would walk into these sessions at 7 p.m. exhausted and tired after working 12 hour days and amazingly, time after time, I would leave energized, fueled, and ready to take on the world.

It finally hit me! I had discovered my passion. Speaking and training to help other people grow.

I believe we are all placed on this earth for a special purpose and it is up to us to find out what that purpose is. Unfortunately, most people never even begin by asking the question, "What is my purpose in life?"

May I invite you to join me as we begin a journey to help you (discover two things):

1. What you will look like in your new skin?
2. What strategies you will use to get there?

WARNING!

THE FOLLOWING SECTION MAY SHOCK YOU.

TAKE A DEEP BREATH AND TURN THE PAGE IF YOU ARE READY TO SHED!

SHEDDING STRATEGIES

E arlier in the book I mentioned one of my goals was to learn from everyone in life. Throughout my career as an ER nurse, psychiatric nurse, administrator and now a consultant, I have met many types of people in many types of situations. I have gone from bedpans to boardrooms...from helping bottom level drunks to top level CEO's.

It's interesting that we are all not that different. We all have very similar problems, issues and core needs. We are all human. And it is in that humanness that we learn.

Every person we meet, every situation we encounter, every challenge we meet, every idea we hear, every emotion we experience is a gift. It is the same for all of us. At first glance, it may not look like one, especially the ones wrapped in brown paper bags. But the gift is there for us to receive and learn from if we choose.

"What have you learned today?" has been my mantra for years. No matter what happens, no matter who I meet, I ask, "what can I learn?"

The unconventional strategies that follow are provided to help you shed. Some of you might say the intent is to shock. You may be right. But, more so, my desire is to teach, to help you think and grow, and to help you look at skills from a different perspective.

The ideas shared have been developed from various means—observing maladaptive behaviors, questioning conventional wisdom, personal experience. Everyone has strengths and skills. Any strength over-used can become your greatest weakness. From every idea seeps truth. It is up to us to find the morsel.

My hope is that you consider what you can learn from everyone, every behavior, every experience that you encounter. To help facilitate that change you will find a 60 second challenge that demands your participation. In addition, lizard factoids are interspersed to test your knowledge along the way.

"Everything that happens to you is your teacher.
The secret is to learn to sit at the feet of
your own life and be taught by it."
Polly B. Berends, Author

#1
BE PSYCHOTIC!

Yes, I said "Be Psychotic!" Don't deal with reality. Get into your own little world. Come on, just take a breather. You deserve a mental breakdown. Get out your calendar and let's schedule it now! After all you have been through, you've earned it. Besides, life is way too stressful to deal with reality all of the time! Think about it, if you were psychotic you wouldn't have to deal with all those mounting bills, the demanding bosses, the irate customers, the challenging teenagers!!

By now, about 50% of you are thinking I have lost my mind and asking yourself why I would suggest something so crazy. The other 50% of you are thinking that this might be a viable option, at least for a brief period of time!

Okay, Okay, Okay...the reality is that we can't live in a psychotic world, even though it may seem at times like a great escape from life's problems. But that doesn't mean we can't borrow aspects of psychosis to help us shed.

After working in psychiatric units for many years I have had many occasions to observe psychosis. One of the common characteristics, as many of you know, is that psychotic people hear voices. They hear voices that tell them to do things. Many of the people listen to the voices.

So, what can we learn from being psychotic?

Well, within each of us is a voice, an inner voice that speaks to us. Most of the time that voice speaks our truth. Some people call it "your gut," some people call it their sixth sense, but it is that voice that comes from within. It is that voice that tells you to take the job, not to marry the guy, to pick up the phone and call someone. It's that inner gnaw that says (sometimes screams) "Stop! Something is wrong" or "yes, do it!"

The challenge is that most of us with our busy lives do not stop long enough to take a deep breath, let alone listen to our inner voice. I wonder, if you did, what would your inner voice say?

Listening to your inner voice is 100% your choice! Shed or You're Dead*!

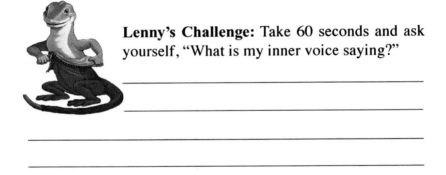

Lenny's Challenge: Take 60 seconds and ask yourself, "What is my inner voice saying?"

_____

_____

_____

_____

"Do not follow the ideas of others,
but learn to listen to the voice within yourself.
Your body and mind will become clear and
you will realize the unity of all things."

Dogen, Zen Master

#2
BE EMOTIONAL!

Be emotional! Let it all out! Don't worry who is watching. Scream! Get excited! Yell!

Imagine you get tickets to attend one of the most popular game shows on TV for the past 30 years. Drew Carey (yes, they SHED Bob Barker) is on the stage and you hear "COME ON DOWN...you are the next contestant on *The Price is Right*!"

You jump from your seat, scream, run down the aisle, dash up the stairs, grab Drew and pick him up and twirl him around!! You start to scream, "I can't believe I am here!" (As Drew is bobbing up and down, don't you just know he is thinking, "They are not paying me enough to do this?")

Okay, Okay, Okay...Reality is we can't be going around all the time letting all our emotions out. So, what can we learn from being emotional?

PASSION!

The dictionary defines passion as a deep intense powerful emotion such as love, joy, hate or anger. One of life's most basic questions is, "Why am I here?" What is your purpose on earth? A good place to start is to ask yourself about your passions. What creates energy for you, both positively and negatively?

On a recent flight to Salt Lake City, I overheard two businessmen talking in the seats next to me. With a deep sigh, one man said to the other, "Just ten more years and I can retire and do what I really want to do with my life."

What a shame! Life is too short!

Frederick Buechner, philosopher, said, "To find our calling is to find the intersection between our deep gladness and the world's deep hunger."

Following your passion, your calling in life, is one of the most important things you will ever do!

Living your passion is 100% your choice!
Shed or You're Dead*!

Lenny's Challenge: Take 60 seconds and ask yourself, "What are the things or activities that create energy for me? What drains my energy?" Write them down.

Creates Energy   Drains Energy

_____   _____

_____   _____

_____   _____

_____   _____

How do those things fit into your job?

_____

_____

_____

"Don't die with your music inside of you!"
Dr. Wayne Dyer, Psychologist, Author

#3
HALLUCINATE!

Yes, Hallucinate! Can't you see those bugs crawling up the wall? Grab them. Call the exterminator NOW! Hurry, before they take over the house!

Okay, Okay, Okay…maybe there aren't REALLY insects swarming your house. Maybe you just saw one ladybug sitting on the ledge outside the window.

So, what in the world can we learn from hallucinating?

My experience as a psychiatric nurse allowed me to also observe people hallucinating. As some of you know, hallucinating patients see, hear, and feel things that are not real. The often visualize people and objects that are not really there but they talk and act as if they were.

People who hallucinate have the ability to visualize. What if you could take that attribute, seeing things that aren't there (visualization) and consciously apply it to your life? It could be one of the most powerful tools for personal transformation.

In 1996, I attended a national health care meeting where Scott Adams, creator of Dilbert, was the opening keynote speaker. As I sat there with 15,000 other people, I heard him share how he had become a national syndicated cartoonist. Years ago, he was a mid-level manager sitting in a cubicle within a huge corporation. He had a dream to become a nationally syndicated cartoonist.

He shared with the audience that he decided to write "SCOTT ADAMS IS A NATIONALLY SYNDICATED CARTOONIST" 15 times a day, just like it was a reality. He went on to say that everyday he would get up, write his sentences and before he knew it, his visualization became true! (If you don't believe him, just open up your newspaper and read his daily cartoon in the funnies section!)

I leaned over and sarcastically said to the person next to me, "Yea, right...that's ridiculous!"

Eight months later, I was in my office and stumbled upon my notes from the conference under some papers on my desk. I glanced down and reread "SCOTT ADAMS IS A NATIONALLY SYNDICATED CARTOONIST, 15 TIMES A DAY."

"It just couldn't work," I said to myself, "How could it?" Later that week, I decided I would prove Scott Adams and his crazy idea wrong.

I had a dream to become a national speaker and author. I thought, "would that be a good sentence to write?" And if Scott Adams wrote sentences 15 times a day, let's do five more for good luck...I'll write 20!" Besides, I was the master of writing sentences in school. I must have written I WILL NOT TALK IN CLASS about 50,000 times! I had even devised a way to take apart a four-color pen and write four sentences at a time! (If anyone needs coaching on this skill, please contact me!)

The test was on...
Two sentences 20 times a day.

Kathy Dempsey is a national speaker.
Kathy Dempsey is an author.

Well, I am here to tell you that 10,000 sentences later, both of those statements came true! What happen? I programmed my unconscious. It didn't know reality from fiction.

If you can visualize it, it will happen!

Visualizing your future is 100% your choice! Shed or You're Dead*!

Lenny's Challenge: Take 60 seconds and ask yourself, "What is the sentence that I will write?" What is your visualization? Write the sentence below as if it was already true. (Go ahead, write it four times!)

_____

_____

_____

_____

"The only difference between a hallucination and a vision is the number of people who see it."
Terry Paulson Ph.D., Psychologist and Author

43

#4
BE BLUNT!

Yes, be blunt! Tell it like it is! Spare no one's feelings. "Sam that is the ugliest tie I have ever seen! Don't tell me you paid money for that!"

Okay, Okay, Okay...maybe we can't just blurt out EVERYTHING we think! And being too blunt can hurt the feelings of others. So, what is the morsel we learn from being blunt?

Most of us have had occasion to observe people who tell it like it is. They don't mess around with trying to sugarcoat anything! They are candid, forthright straight shooters, sometimes so painfully honest, it stings.

This reminds me of a cold winter morning several years ago. It was 6 a.m. when I hopped in my car and left Chattanooga heading to Atlanta for a National Speakers Association meeting. As I pulled off the freeway exit ramp, I noticed a man sitting on an old egg crate box on the side of the road.

The man was wrapped tightly in a dirty old plaid jacket, brown knit hat, black gloves and a red wool scarf. He was bundled up so snugly that I could barely see his eyes.

As I approached the stoplight, I looked down and saw a sign he was fighting to keep up against the wind. It read, "I'll be honest, I want beer." I did a double take and read the sign again.

This man was a beggar attempting to blatantly elicit money from the drivers exiting off the ramp so he could go buy beer. I was shocked when the car in front of me stopped and threw in a few bills into his shoe box.

A variety of emotions flooded my mind. Most of them, I must admit, were negative. Why would anybody stop and give money to someone who admitted they were going to buy beer instead of food to sustain themselves?

As I drove into the parking garage at the meeting site one thought kept blaring out. This guy was honest! I might not have respected anything else about the man but at least he was honest...with himself and with others.

The blunt person can teach us to tell it like it is. All too often we refuse to be honest with ourselves and others. When we are not honest, everybody loses. And until we can face the truth, sometimes the brutal truth, we can't move on in our growth.

Being honest is 100% your choice!
Shed or You're Dead°!

 **Lenny's Challenge:** Take 60 seconds and ask yourself, "What is something that has been holding me back? Maybe something I need to be honest with myself about my life, my work, or my relationships?"

_____

_____

_____

"Our lives improve only when we take chances —
and the first and most difficult risk we can take
is to be honest with ourselves."
Walter Anderson, Artist

#5
Be Obsessive!

Yes, be obsessive! Check the stove, check the iron, and scrub that floor, again and again and again! In fact, go ahead and turn back to page one and start reading this book over again!

By the way, when was the last time you washed your hands? Do you realize how many germs you have picked up in the last few minutes handling this book?

Okay, Okay, Okay, Okay, Okay, Okay, being obsessive over and over again will only drive everyone crazy including you. So, what can we learn from being obsessive?

People who obsess have a few challenges in life. I must admit, I have been accused of being OCD (Obsessive Compulsive Disorder) more than once in my life but I'm nothing like my sister and brother-in-law! Even their cleaning lady complains because she can't find anything to do when she gets to their house!

Besides their ability to create order, one of the OCD gifts is their ability to focus—an ability to hyper-focus on things. They have a tendency to have a one-track mind. They have their focus and no matter what it takes, they will do what they need to do!

This one-track mind syndrome reminds me of an experience I had a few years ago.

"*Hercules*, the new Disney movie, opens this Friday night" the advertisement in the local paper announced. I was so excited! I had seen the previews for months and Friday night couldn't get here soon enough.

One problem. This was a kid's movie. As a well respected administrator in the community, this could potentially be very embarrassing.

After further contemplation, I decided I needed a cover. So, I called my nephew Trey, then 6 years old, to go with me. No one would ever suspect I was actually the one who wanted to see the movie; they would just think I was an awesome aunt.

Friday night came and Trey and I were the first in line for the 7 p.m. show. As we walked out of the theater after the movie, I was stunned. This was a wonderful movie. I was struck with what a powerful story it was and how many significant life lessons it contained. How did Hercules become a hero? He was obsessed with his goal! What was his plan? He was obsessed with being a hero! How did he do it? By being obsessed with his goal!

I couldn't get the impact of the movie out of my mind. I was so intrigued that when I got home that evening, I got on line, found Hercules on the web and sent him an email. Believe it or not, but he actually responded.

Dear Kathy,

Thanks for inquiring about my journey and the strategies I used to become a hero. Let me share with you my four point plan.

1. I had a dream. I had a dream and I believed in that dream. I found my passion in life; I discovered my true purpose.

2. I found a coach. I didn't know how to become a hero. I needed someone to teach me. I needed someone to believe in me. I needed someone to support and encourage me. Phil, at first, had no interest in being my coach. But I was determined because he was the best, and I wouldn't give up until he said yes. Phil helped me

be accountable to myself and to my goals.

3. I overcame barriers. Pain and Panic, who often disguised themselves as my friends, continually tried to destroy me. As much as I tried to deny their existence, I finally had to realize that I had to learn to cope and live with both of them throughout my life. I learned how to control what I had control over and let go of the rest.

4. I stayed focused. I had to continually remind myself of my goal. Life continually hits us with distractions. I soon realized I could not let them get me off track. I had to prioritize and stay focused on my goal.

Kathy, I hope my response is helpful to you. My only request is that you share it with others as they strive to reach their goals in life.

Sincerely,
Mr. Hercules

Developing laser focus is 100% your choice!
Shed or You're Dead*!

Lenny's Challenge: Take 60 seconds and ask yourself, "What is one thing that I need to develop laser focus in my life right now?"

_____

_____

_____

"If you chase two rabbits, both will escape."
Anonymous

Lizard Factoid #1

In order to protect itself from a predator, a lizard will do what?

    A. Hiss at them.

    B. Bite them.

    C. Self-amputate their tails.

    D. Spray them with mace.

(Answer on next page)

Correct answer: C

Lizards have the ability to self amputate their tails for protection. The process is known as *autotomy*. Here's what happens. The tail bones have a special weak spot where a contraction of the muscles at that point causes the bone to break and the tail to become loose. The lizard smacks its tail on the ground and it snaps off. The separated tail continues to wriggle for several minutes which holds the attention of the predator while the now tail-less lizard makes its escape. Believe it or not, but the lizard will actually grow a new tail!

Oh, so that explains it...

We, as humans, must also learn to detach. And the lizard reminds us how important detachment is for survival. We may often wonder how detachment can be healthy, but sometimes it is necessary to separate ourselves from others or things that may ultimately destroy us or inhibit our growth.

Detaching from things that inhibit personal growth is 100% your choice! Shed or You're Dead*!

#6
BE A CRY BABY!

Yes, be a cry baby! Whine, scream, and cry until you cry yourself to sleep! You spilled your milk, oh, no, cry about it! Where are you going to get more milk? You didn't get the promotion you wanted, go ahead, and throw a temper tantrum. Yell at your kids, kick the dog. Why not go out to a bar and drown yourself in your sorrows?

Okay, Okay, Okay...crying about everything probably isn't the best way to cope. So, what can we learn from being a cry baby?

We can learn to grieve our losses. Most of us have been told not to cry over spilled milk. You know what? It is okay to cry over it. You lost something. And all losses must be appropriately grieved. You can't stuff it...well, you can, but if you don't deal with it now, it will come out. Trust me, it will come out in some way...physically, emotionally, financially, spiritually.

In my many years of taking care of psychiatric patients, I discovered that most of them, when you look at their core issues, were hospitalized because they had never cried over spilled milk. They had losses that they had stuffed, some of them for many years. Unfortunately, the grief couldn't be stuffed any longer and had reared its ugly head in drug and alcohol addictions, physical and emotional diseases, financial failures, and broken relationships.

It's okay to cry, even you men who are reading this! It's actually healthy. Crying is the body's way of healing itself. Healthy grieving includes allowing yourself an appropriate time to grieve over a loss and developing healthy coping mechanisms to channel the emotions.

Grieving your losses is 100% your choice!
Shed or You're Dead*!

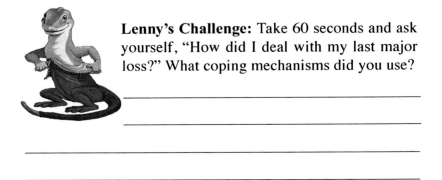

Lenny's Challenge: Take 60 seconds and ask yourself, "How did I deal with my last major loss?" What coping mechanisms did you use?

_____

_____

_____

_____

"Grief is like a desert, and the
only way out of it is through it."
Rita Barclay, Insightful Human

#7
BE PESSIMISTIC!

Yes, be pessimistic! Come on, think negative! What is the use in trying? You know that life is always going to be the same: the rich will get richer and the poor will get poorer. Nothing in life is certain except for death and taxes. Why take a chance and do anything different?

I have an idea. You can be the poster child for Mr. Murphy! You remember his law, "If anything can go wrong, it will!" Make your life motto, "Expect the worst," then you will never be disappointed!

Okay, Okay, Okay, maybe being negative is not the best way to think. I am feeling down just writing about it. So, what can we learn from being pessimistic?

Pessimistic people are constantly thinking, what if, what if, what if. They tend to be negative, worst case scenario people. They always see the glass as half empty. These are the type of people who say, "I never get a break!" just after they win the $100 million lottery. "If only I had waited a couple more days, it would have doubled!"

Pessimistic people have developed the skill of looking at the worst and they do it very well (just a little too much).

When faced with life's challenges, it is often helpful to take a moment (JUST ONE MOMENT) and ask what the worst thing that could happen would be. Sometimes we catastrophize and think the sky is falling. Once you are able to identify the worse case scenario, it enables you to move on. Frequently, the worst thing that could happen is not always as bad or realistic as we think.

Planning for the worst is 100% your choice!
Shed or You're Dead*!

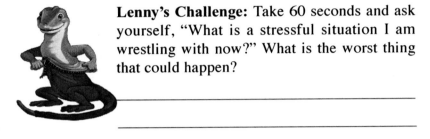

Lenny's Challenge: Take 60 seconds and ask yourself, "What is a stressful situation I am wrestling with now?" What is the worst thing that could happen?

_____

_____

_____

_____

"Having reckoned what to do in the
worst possible circumstances, when better arise,
as they may, life becomes child's play."

Thomas Hardy, English Novelist and Poet

#8
BE A POLLYANNA!

Yes, be Pollyanna! Everything will work out. Don't worry. I can see it now, your ship is about to come in! Nothing can go wrong! Oh, don't forget to put on those rose colored glasses!

Okay, Okay, Okay...maybe we can't live in that rose colored dream world. (Although it sure would be nice to, wouldn't it?)

For those of you who don't remember the story of Pollyanna (from 1913) she was an orphan who went to live with her harsh maiden aunt. Soon, all the sad, the lonely, the sick, and the obnoxious in town became enamored with Pollyanna's enthusiasm, zeal, and infectious optimism about life.

Today, unfortunately, being called a Pollyanna is considered a derogatory comment meaning he or she is not living in reality.

Pollyanna reminds me of the old story of the boy on Christmas Day going to the barn. All he finds are piles of manure. He immediately jumps up and down, smiles, and screams, "With all this manure, there must be a pony around here somewhere!"

So, what can we learn from being a Pollyanna?

When faced with difficult life challenges, it is helpful to look at what the best thing that could happen might be, especially when we are buried deep in the "manure experiences" of life and can't imagine there is a way out.

So next time your life seems like it is surrounded with manure be Pollyanna for a moment and think of the possibilities. Guess what? There is probably a pony and some other wonderful things just waiting for you to find them! (Remember, sometimes it may take a little digging!)

Expecting the best is 100% your choice!
Shed or You're Dead*!

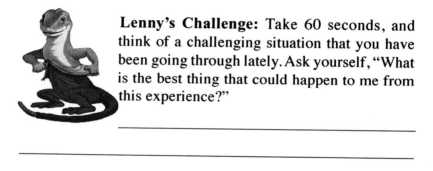

Lenny's Challenge: Take 60 seconds, and think of a challenging situation that you have been going through lately. Ask yourself, "What is the best thing that could happen to me from this experience?"

_____

_____

_____

_____

"Some people are always grumbling because roses have thorns. I am thankful that thorns have roses."

Allophones Karr, Wise Person

#9
BROWN NOSE!

Yes, brown nose people every opportunity you can! Tell them how wonderful they look, how impressed you are to meet them. What an awesome person they are! I LOVE THAT TIE!! Remember the old classic TV show, *Leave it to Beaver*? Make Eddie Haskell your role model!

Okay, Okay, Okay…maybe Eddie Haskell would not be the first person you should model behavior after. So, what can learn we learn from being a brown noser?

I am sure you have observed people who have achieved their Ph.D. in brown-nosing. They have developed this skill very well and continually look for every possible opportunity they can find to tell you something positive about yourself. They have a mindset that is constantly focused on asking, "How can I compliment someone else?"

The question that most people wonder when they encounter brown nosers is, "Are they being sincere?" And some of the time, the answer is that their intentions are not totally above board and honest. Sincerity or insincerity? Therein lies the issue.

Harvard University conducted a study looking at self-esteem. They discovered that in order to build and maintain a healthy sense of self-esteem, children need at least 15 positive statements a day. They also found out that adults need at least five.

Wouldn't it be wonderful to constantly focus your energy on catching people doing something right, and praising them for it! Think about what five positive statements a day would do for a person, let alone 10 or 15? Holy cow, think about what 20 would do? When you SINCERELY encourage others, everyone wins!

Building other's self-esteem is 100% your choice! Shed or You're Dead*!

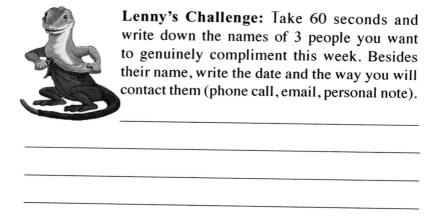

Lenny's Challenge: Take 60 seconds and write down the names of 3 people you want to genuinely compliment this week. Besides their name, write the date and the way you will contact them (phone call, email, personal note).

_____

_____

_____

_____

"I can live for two months on a good compliment."
Mark Twain, Great American Author

#10
DON'T WEAR CLEAN UNDERWEAR!

Yes, don't wear clean underwear! Now some of you must be thinking, "I can't believe she just said that." For those of you who are shocked and are doubting yourself for really paying money for this book, please stay with me for just a moment. Don't close the book yet.

I know what your mom probably told you. At least I know what my mom told me. "Always wear clean underwear." I am having a flashback now. I've grabbed my lunch and am running out the door and mom says, "Kathy, are you wearing clean underwear? You never know if you are going to be in an accident."

Mom was right. You never know...

But reality is that the chances of you actually being in an accident and going to the ER are less than 1%. (Let me just say, if you were in an accident, you probably wouldn't still have clean underwear on when you finally got to the ER.)

I hear some of you agreeing with my statistic and still wondering what's the lesson here? What can we learn from not wearing clean underwear (other than less wasted time doing laundry)?

Most of us spend time worrying about things that never happen. Did you know that 90% of the things we worry about never happen? And yet, we spend countless hours and enormous amounts of energy worrying about things that usually never occur. If something does happen, you deal with it. Worrying about it never helps!

Okay, Okay, Okay...I am not honestly suggesting you NEVER wear clean underwear, but you might be happier and healthier if you don't worry about all the "what if's" so much.

PS: Kathy began her career as an ER nurse and she wants everyone to know that they are NOT UNDERWEAR INSPECTORS. Well, not much! (Now that Kathy is thinking about it, she did have a lot of patients named Calvin Klein!)

> ### Worrying is 100% your choice!
> ### Shed or You're Dead*!

 **Lenny's Challenge:** Take 60 seconds and ask yourself, "What is something in my work or personal life that I have been worrying about lately? Can I do anything about it? If so, what action will I take today, instead of worrying, to address the issue." If you can't do anything, then let it go.

Emergency First Aid: If you get into worry attack, take 60 seconds and concentrate all your efforts on worrying about this single problem. Go ahead. NOW! WORRY 'til your little heart is 60 seconds content! Then, commit to yourself to taking the rest of the day off and not worrying about this problem. If you feel yourself slipping back, look at your watch and allow yourself another 60 seconds to worry about the problem then refocus back on your day.

> "Worry is like a rocking chair—it gives you
> something to do but it doesn't get you anywhere."
> Dorothy Galyean, Author

Lizard Factoid #2

If you notice a shedding problem with a lizard, what is the best thing to do?

A. Just wait, the lizard may get better on its own.

B. Feed the lizard, it must be hungry.

C. Search through and analyze the lizard's environment and diet.

D. Pop some popcorn, relax and watch Jurassic Park.

(Answer on next page)

Correct Answer: C

A lizard's shedding problem is a sign of a greater, underlying issue. When a shedding problem occurs, the best thing to do is to search and seek out information by investigating and analyzing the lizard's environment, diet and social life.

So, that explains it...

For humans, life hands us many opportunities to shed. With every change, we potentially can get stuck and have problems shedding. In order to facilitate a healthy shed, the first thing to do is to search, ask questions and gather information.

**Healthy shedding is 100% your choice!
Shed or You're Dead*!**

#11
BE A KNOW-IT-ALL!

Yes, be a know-it-all! Say good-bye to school! Don't study. Goof off. Consider yourself smart enough. You don't need to learn anything else. You are the expert! You know it all already. Don't even think about clogging up your brain with one more piece of useless information!

Okay, Okay, Okay...being a know-it-all may not be the smartest thing for your britches! So, what can we learn from these "experts?"

Well, the know-it-all, to some extent, values knowledge. They may not be the experts they think they are but they do try to communicate to everyone around them that they know "it."

So, how can we continue to value knowledge? Many people set their goal to graduate from school with a degree. All too often, the goal is to get the diploma and tragically some forget about the real purpose—learning. Many finish school and consciously stop learning.

Bob Pike, a dear friend and mentor says, "Learning has not taken place until behavior has changed." We may pass the test, get the diploma, the Ph.D., but unless our behavior changes, have we really learned anything or do we just have a certificate to hang on our wall?

Peter Senge, author of *The Fifth Discipline* and an MIT management guru, often proclaims that in the future, learners will be the only ones that survive and thrive!

My ritual at the end of every day is to ask myself the question, "What have I learned today?" I have discovered that if

I haven't learned anything, I am not growing. I am not shedding. And shedding means acting on what you've learned!

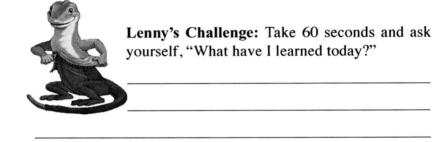

Being a life-long learner is 100% your choice!
Shed or You're Dead*!

Lenny's Challenge: Take 60 seconds and ask yourself, "What have I learned today?"

_____

_____

_____

_____

"Every experience in life offers an opportunity for learning. The smartest people are those who can transform the smallest event or situation into breakthroughs in thinking and action."

Gary Ryan Blair, Author, Speaker

#12
LOSE YOUR MEMORY!

Yes, lose your memory! Forget everything you know! Don't try those accelerated learning techniques and memory power aids, they will just clog up your mind with lots of useless information!

Okay, Okay, Okay...maybe it's not a good idea to forget everything. So, what can we learn from losing our memory? Why in the world would we even consider such a crazy thought?

Quite possibly a number of reasons.

I worked for several years as the administrator of an Alzheimer's Day Care Center. One day, I walked over to meet with the director of the center. As I passed through the hospital corridor I immediately thought of my mom, who had spent many days and nights at the hospital before she ultimately died from cancer. Tears came to my eyes as I thought about all the pain and suffering she went through and how desperately I wished she was still alive.

Immediately, upon entering the center I was enthusiastically greeted by Emma, one of the clients who was wiping off the dining room table. I had never seen anyone clean a table so intensely. Laughing with the other clients, I observed Emma go back again and rub the table to make sure it was spotless.

"Emma," I said, "You have been cleaning the table several times and it looks great. How are you doing today?"

She smiled as she glanced up from the table, "I am losing my memory. I can't remember anything. I don't know what I did yesterday, I don't know what I am going to do tomorrow, all I can focus on is this moment, on being happy and doing the best job I can do. Is there anything I can help you do?"

Wow! Emma taught me a powerful lesson that day. Living in the moment. She didn't have a choice. Emma had to live in the moment because disease had tragically taken her memory away.

The gift of memory can be a curse if we allow it to be. Tragically, at times, we allow our memories to rob us of the present. Sometimes it may be helpful to consciously forget painful or unpleasant events that serve no purpose other than to bring us down and take our minds off the present. "Conscious forgetting" may serve us all well!

> **Living in the present is 100% your choice!**
> **Shed or You're Dead***!

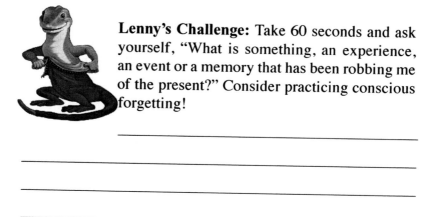

Lenny's Challenge: Take 60 seconds and ask yourself, "What is something, an experience, an event or a memory that has been robbing me of the present?" Consider practicing conscious forgetting!

_____

_____

_____

_____

"Happiness is good health and a bad memory!"
Ingrid Bergman, Actress

#13
EAT TWO CRICKETS A DAY!

Yes, eat bugs! Are you crazy? No, I am suggesting you eat bugs! You can find them at your local pet store. (You can even buy them on line at www.PetSmart.com. (Don't worry I am not getting any profits from this plug!!)

Recently, I was working with a pest control company and was talking with an entomologist (that would be a bug doctor). I told her I had heard that America is the only civilization that does not eat insects.

She said, "Actually, that is not true. We all eat bugs every day." She went on to say, "I know this may be hard to swallow (no pun intended), but the government has standards on the percentage of bug parts that food companies can allow in their food."

Doesn't that make you feel good right now? Thinking of a quick trip to a garbage can? Need a Delta Air Lines barf bag?

Okay, Okay, Okay...I can tell I am loosing a few of you now. So what can we learn from eating bugs? My childhood pediatrician taught me an incredible lesson.

It was 5:30 a.m. when I rushed out the door in my sweats to head for the gym. As I flew into the woman's locker room I ran into Dr. Minnie Vance, my favorite childhood doctor. Everyone loved Dr. Vance. I wished she could have been my doctor for life. (I actually tried that for as long as I could. I was 22 years old, sitting in the doctor's office, in those tiny little chairs, waiting for my physical for nursing school. When they called my name and asked, "Where is your child?" I knew this was reality telling me it was time to grow up and find an adult doctor.)

But Dr. Vance was and still is my hero. She is what I want to be when I am 72 years old.

She looked down at my "Shed or You're Dead®" lizard t-shirt and defiantly said, "Kathy, you need to eat two crickets a day to shed your skin!"

Taken back that my doctor would advise me to eat crickets, I chuckled and with a grimace said, "Yuk!" Just the mental image of ingesting a cricket made me sick.

She smiled and responded, "I am serious. Yesterday I bought a week's supply of 14 crickets for my granddaughter's lizard. I know crickets don't sound appetizing but sometimes the things we need to do in life are not palatable, yet healthy and needed."

I jumped on the gym's treadmill and thought about how Dr. Vance was right. What would be my two crickets a day? What are the two things that I need to do in order to shed my skin and grow? For me, the answer was journaling and exercise.

"Two crickets every day in order to shed skin." That is the strangest, yet most insightful, prescription I had ever heard. Maybe we all should consider this doctor's order!

Nurturing yourself daily is 100% your choice!
Shed or You're Dead*!

68

Lenny's Challenge: Take 60 seconds and ask yourself, "What are my two crickets, the two things I need to do everyday in order to shed my skin and help me grow?"

_____

_____

_____

_____

"Two bugs a day keeps the doctor away!"
Lenny's Cousin Louie

#14
MAKE MISTAKES!

Go ahead. Make mistakes. Lots of them! Screw up! Fail! Fall flat on your face! Don't worry about learning from them. You have plenty of erasers. Feel free to repeat the same mistakes over and over and over again.

Okay, Okay, Okay...you don't have to intentionally set out to make lots of mistakes. So, what can we learn from making mistakes?

Ask Thomas Edison, who discovered the light bulb. After 1,000 unsuccessful attempts with no luck, someone asked him why he kept going after so many failures. He said, "I haven't failed. I have figured out 1,000 ways it doesn't work."

Failure is on the path to success. One of my mentors told me if I wasn't experiencing failure, I probably wasn't taking enough risk and stretching myself to reach my full potential.

After conducting research with hundreds of people about what their number one barrier to shedding and growth is, fear of failure tops the list.

Every highly successful person I know, when asked about their journey, has made some mistakes along the way. Some of them have experienced huge failures. The challenge is to take the risk and allow yourself to make mistakes, to learn from them and keep going!

All of us will make some bad decisions in life. They key is what we learn from them. What will we do different tomorrow? Will we make the same mistake?

**Learning from your failures is 100% your choice!
Shed or You're Dead°!**

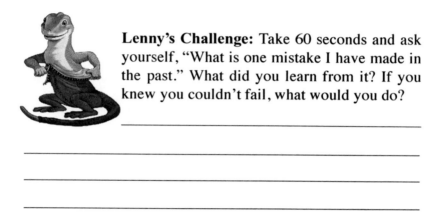

Lenny's Challenge: Take 60 seconds and ask yourself, "What is one mistake I have made in the past." What did you learn from it? If you knew you couldn't fail, what would you do?

_____

_____

_____

_____

"A failure is not a failure unless you
don't learn from it."

Mr. Ernest O. Bleuer, Kathy's Dad

#15
DON'T CONSERVE!

Don't conserve your resources! Burn more fuel! Use more water! Spend more money. Don't worry about eating everything on your plate, the food will never get to those starving children in China anyway!?

Okay, Okay, Okay...maybe we should consider recycling those coke cans. So, what can we learn from not being conservative?

People who are not conservationists don't spend time thinking about how to save the planet. They do whatever it takes to get and use the resources they need. If it's money, they spend it; if it's fuel, they burn it; if it's water, they use it; if it's food, they waste it. No holding back!

People who don't conserve, utilize. They use whatever possible resources they have. When they run out, they are masters in discovering creative ways of finding more.

How can we look at using all the resources available to us?

Ready, set, go! The competition was on. I had challenged the group to choose a common object (coat hanger, vase, phone cord, toilet paper) from the table and take three minutes to come up with as many different uses for the object as they could.

"Time's up!" I declared.

I was shocked to discover that the winning team had come up with 83 different uses for toilet paper!

Note paper, scarf, bandage, underwear, breast enhancer... WOW! Who would have ever thought toilet paper could have so many potential uses?

In our daily lives we have so many resources around us. Often, we fail to stop and identify them, especially when we are in crisis or going through a challenging time.

Resources come in many different forms: finances, friends, family, churches, community services, internal skills.

Utilizing your resources is 100% your choice! Shed or You're Dead*!

Lenny's Challenge: Take 60 seconds and list out as many uses for a coat hanger, vase, or phone cord as you can. Which one did you choose?

Ready, Set, Go!

_____

_____

_____

_____

_____

_____

_____

_____

Great! Now here is Lenny's second challenge, take another 60 seconds and ask yourself, "How many resources can I identify in my life?"

_____

_____

_____

_____

_____

_____

_____

_____

_____

"Most people have no idea of the giant capacity
we can immediately command when we focus all of
our resources on mastering a single area of our lives."

Anthony Robbins, Motivational Speaker and Author

Lizard Factoid #3

Right before a lizard sheds, what happens?

A. It descends into the ground and hides.

B. It changes colors and its eyes become impaired with a cloudy substance.

C. It loses its appetite and gets cranky.

D. All of the above.

(Answer on next page)

Correct Answer: D, all of the above.

Before a shed a lizard will often descend to the ground where it needs to hide as the shedding process starts. The lizard begins to change colors, becoming dimmer and duller. Its eyes are impaired as the old lenses cloud over making it difficult for them to see. Many lizards lose their appetite and get cranky.

Oh, so that explains it…

Shedding is a very disorienting time for lizards and for humans. Our moods change, we can't see anything clearly and sometimes we retreat and isolate ourselves. All those behaviors are normal reactions when we are going through a growth period. But it is critical that if a successful shed is to occur that you commit to helping yourself, that you are honest with yourself and others, and that you get help and support when needed.

**Successful shedding is 100% your choice!
Shed or You're Dead*!**

#16
GET ANGRY!

Yes, Get mad. Let it all out! Your boss ticked you off by giving the promised promotion to someone else. Explode! Go home and kick the dog! Yell and scream at the kids #!#!#!#!#!#! Your spouse ticked you off...go ahead, slam the door, give them the silent treatment, paybacks are Hell!

Okay, Okay, Okay...it might not be the best idea to let it all hang out, especially if you want to keep your job and stay married. So, what can we learn from people that get angry?

Angry people get mad. They are internally fuelled with raging emotions. The question is, is it okay to be angry?

Yes, anger is okay! Some of us, especially women, received a strong message growing up that anger is wrong. It was not okay. It was inappropriate. Unfortunately, many of us never learned how to appropriately express our feelings. Conversely, many men learned the opposite; you fought it out when you were angry.

Anger is not only okay, it is healthy and a necessary part of shedding, of dealing with loss. It's how we are able to grieve and go on. Of all the challenges to shedding, I have found many people get stuck in this stage. They don't know what to do with the anger. They either let it explode or they stuff it and it comes out in other ways.

If you don't learn to control your anger, someone else will. Many criminals in our prisons today are there because they never learned how to appropriately deal with anger. When someone ticked them off, they just went out and shot them, or hurt them in some way. So much of the violence we have in our schools directly relates back to kids not knowing how to express their angry feelings.

The key to dealing with anger is that you acknowledge the feelings and learn how to appropriately deal with them. Verbally expressing your feelings is critical. Sublimation is essential.

In fact, sublimation is one of the healthiest coping strategies you can use—channeling the negative energy to more appropriate avenues. Exercise, hobbies, journaling, what ever works for you. It is important that you have a game plan to deal with anger before it hits you.

> **Expressing your feelings appropriately**
> **is 100% your choice!**
> **Shed or You're Dead*!**

Lenny's Challenge: Take 60 seconds and ask yourself, "How do I deal with anger now?" What might be two ways in which you could deal with the angry negative feelings in a healthier way?

_____

_____

_____

_____

"Holding on to anger is like grasping a hot coal
with the intent of throwing it at someone else;
you are the one who gets burned."
Buddha

#17
BUG PEOPLE!

Yes, Bug People! Annoy them! Can you help me? Please? What should I say? How do I do it? Where do I find it? When should I do it? How long should it take? Who else can help me?

Okay, Okay, Okay…keep asking questions and bugging people and you may find someone has called your local pest control service on you! So, what can we learn from bugging people?

Ask questions. Be curious. Don't assume anything. Don't stop until you get the answers. Get the facts!

People who bug people are continually hanging around and asking questions. They won't let you go do what you have to do because they are so focused on getting the answers they need. They seem to have one thing on their mind. Gathering information!

Recently, I had one of those days from Hell, when everything that possibly could go wrong was going wrong. My plane was four hours late, they had lost my luggage, and I was coming down with some bug. What was I going to do? I was scheduled to be at a meeting first thing in the morning to speak. I arrived at the hotel late at night. I was so exhausted that I didn't even speak to the registration clerk. He checked me in, gave me my key, and pointed to the elevator that would take me to the 26th floor.

I dragged my wasted body across the lobby as I staggered onto the elevator which almost closed in my face. When the elevator reached the 26 floor, I stumbled off with two carry-on bags that I was lugging around. Then, I wound around what seemed to be endless hallways, finally reaching my room, 2642.

I pulled the keycard out and placed it in the door. The red light blinked and the door would not open. I tried it again, and again the red light flashed.

"This is the last straw. I can't believe this stupid hotel gave me a key that didn't work," I muttered. I was so mad and tired that I plopped myself down on the floor in the middle of the hallway. I mumbled under my breath, "I'll just sleep here on the floor. Maybe when someone stumbles over me I can get some help."

In my angelic-like (Okay, stubborn) three year old attitude I thought, "I am not budging!" What seemed like ten hours later, in reality was only ten minutes later, a bellman rolled by with his shiny brass luggage cart. He smiled and with a chipper voice said, "May I help you, ma'am?" "It's about time!" I thought to myself.

"Yes, you certainly can! This key doesn't work. I can't get in my room. What kind of hotel is this where you are locked out of your own room?"

I stood up and went to show him. "I am so sorry you are having problems," he said, "let me see what I can do to get you in."

"Can I see your key?" he asked, glancing up from the lock.

With a smug look on my face, I whipped the key out of the door slot and handed it over.

"Ma'am, do you know this key is from the Hilton?"

"Yes, I do!" I replied.

"Well, you are in a Hyatt Hotel," he responded.

My head sunk into my throat as I wished the floor would open up and swallow me. I had been to the Hilton the night before. As I fumbled through my purse and pulled out the actual

Hyatt key the registration clerk had given me, I begged for the bellman's forgiveness.

After my new best friend opened my door with the correct key and carried in my luggage, I collapsed into bed. My lesson in my journal entry that night was BEFORE YOU ACT, GET THE FACTS!

So often, we take situations in our lives and make assumptions, often wrong assumptions without getting the facts, without asking questions!

> **Asking questions and getting the facts is 100% your choice! Shed or You're Dead*!**

 **Lenny's Challenge:** Take 60 seconds and ask yourself, "What is a situation in my life where I need to ask more questions, get more information, and more facts?"

_____

_____

_____

_____

"Just the facts, ma'am. Just the facts."
Joe Friday, Dragnet Sergeant

#18
BE NARCISSISTIC!

Yes, be Narcissistic! Think of yourself! What do YOU want, what do YOU need, that is the real focus in life. What's in it for me!! Come on, YOU are the most important person, why would YOU waste your time or energy on anyone else!

Okay, Okay, Okay…if you kept this up, you may sooner or later get sick and tired of being around yourself. So, what in the world can we learn from being narcissistic?

We can learn to focus on ourselves.

As you know, narcissistic people are self-centered, they think only of themselves. Their needs and how they can get them met is their goal in life. How they might help others is the furthest thing from their mind. The narcissist has it down pat, they can focus on themselves in any situation. No one else does it better!

Last year, a neighbor knocked on my door and asked if she could borrow two eggs for a cake recipe she was attempting to make. Unfortunately, despite my desire to be their friendly neighbor and help the woman out, I could not oblige. I didn't have any eggs to give my neighbor.

(An aside from Lenny: If only the neighbor had known how domestically challenged Kathy was, she never would have stepped foot near Kathy's place. How domestically challenged is she? Let me just say that Kathy did actually set the kitchen on fire by boiling water!)

You can't give what you don't have! If your next door neighbor knocks on your door to borrow an egg, you can't meet their needs unless you have an egg! I had been neglectful in meeting my own needs and had not taken the time from my busy schedule to stop and go to the store to buy eggs in weeks!

Are you selfish about your needs? If not, why not? The more selfish you are about taking the time to get eggs, the more eggs you are going to be able to share with others when they need them. Eggs are one of the basic staples (I know, someone needs to remind me)!

For most of us, thinking about our own needs can be challenging. We are so busy trying to help everyone else that we neglect ourselves. Then we wonder why we are frustrated and exhausted.

Taking care of yourself is 100% your choice!
Shed or You're Dead*!

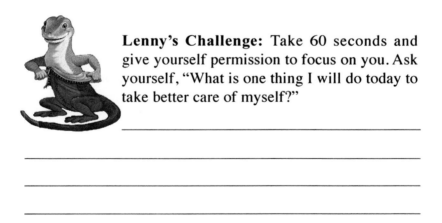

Lenny's Challenge: Take 60 seconds and give yourself permission to focus on you. Ask yourself, "What is one thing I will do today to take better care of myself?"

_____

_____

_____

_____

"In case of emergency, don't forget to place the oxygen mask on yourself, and then assist any minors or others who need assistance."
Delta Flight Attendant

#19
BE IMPULSIVE!

Be impulsive! Yes, right now! Just do it! Don't think about it! Go ahead and buy the new car NOW! You need that new 52" widescreen plasma TV! NOW! Go ahead and take the trip to Maui. NOW! Call — 1-888-I WANT IT! NOW!

Okay, Okay, Okay...don't think anyone (except the credit card companies) thinks that responding impulsively is the best way to live your life. So, what can we learn from being impulsive?

We can learn to make decisions. Impulsive people act. They act quickly, make snap decisions and rarely spend a lot of time thinking about it. They are not known as people who put things off.

Sometimes we have the tendency to get into a syndrome that is often called "analysis paralysis". We follow the path of least resistance and do nothing at all. Not making a decision is really making a decision.

In any situation, it is important to recognize that there are often two different decisions that could be made. First, it may be a situation where you need more information or thoughtful consideration. Or, it could be a situation where you go for it, make the decision, and give it your best shot.

Making timely decisions is 100% your choice!
Shed or You're Dead™!

84

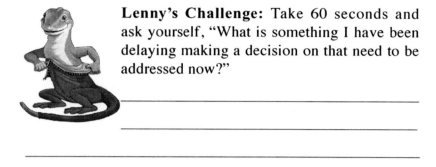

Lenny's Challenge: Take 60 seconds and ask yourself, "What is something I have been delaying making a decision on that need to be addressed now?"

_____

_____

_____

_____

"When you come to a fork in the road, take it!"

Yogi Berra, Baseball Hero

#20
ACT CHILDISH!

Act childish! Yes! Act just like a kid. Throw a temper tantrum! Pick your nose! Wipe your hands on your sleeve! If you don't like what someone did, go ahead and stick your tongue out at them! Call them a name! If you don't get what you want, make yourself feel better by sticking your thumb in your mouth.

Okay, Okay, Okay...maybe sticking your thumb in your mouth is going a bit far. So, what can we learn from being childish?

BE YOURSELF!

Kids have fun. Kids enjoy life. Kids are who they are— themselves! They don't pretend to be someone else. Somehow they haven't been tainted with the "Kathy, you're in public" adult mantra. Most kids are transparent. You know exactly how they are feeling, be it happy, sad, mad, or glad!

All of us were kids, some of us a little longer ago than others. So what happened? Have we been conditioned by adults to be somebody that we are not?

I was reading a true story recently about a guy whose parents wanted him to be a lawyer. From the time he was a small boy, a law career was the expectation. They continued to set that expectation and a few years later the kid grew up and was sent off to Harvard Law School. He graduated at the top of his class just like mom and dad wanted.

He hit it big and was a very successful New York City lawyer. As his practice grew, he continued to have a burning desire to be a teacher. One day, he couldn't take it any longer and decided he had to be true to himself. He quit his multi-million dollar practice and began teaching school for a tenth of the salary. He has now been honored with many national awards for his ability to help others learn.

Remarkably, without all his money and high powered job, he was happier than he had ever been in his life. He was being true to himself. He was enjoying life!

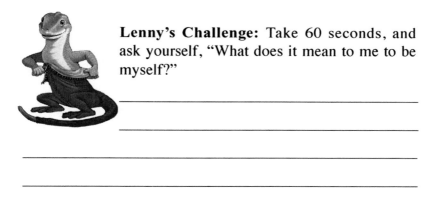

Being yourself is 100% your choice!
Shed or You're Dead*!

Lenny's Challenge: Take 60 seconds, and ask yourself, "What does it mean to me to be myself?"

_____

_____

_____

_____

"The challenge in life is to be yourself in a world that is trying to make you like everyone else."

Anonymous

Lizard Factoid #4

A lizard that sheds quickly is . . . ?

    A. Less likely to be eaten.

    B. More likely to be eaten.

    C. Not in good health.

    D. An Olympic winning lizard.

(Answer on next page)

Correct Answer: A

A lizard that sheds quickly is less likely to be eaten. The most vulnerable time for the lizard is during the shedding process. The quicker it sheds the less vulnerable it is to an attack from prey.

Oh, so that explains it...

Change constantly demands that we shed. The longer we drag out the inevitable shedding process, the more vulnerable we become to getting stuck and consumed by life. How to avoid being eaten in life...decide to shed now! Ready, Set. SHED!

**Healthy shedding is 100% your choice!
Shed or You're Dead·!**

#21
BE CODEPENDENT!

Yes, Be codependent! Where is he? Where is she? You must find a relationship to make your life complete! Hurry, get online and enter to be a contestant on *The Bachelor*! In fact, once you find your soul mate, get totally involved, obsessed, neglect your old friends. You need no one else in life. You and your partner are one!

Okay, Okay, Okay…maybe being enmeshed is not the best relationship. So, what in the world can we learn from being codependent?

Recognizing that in life we all need each other. We need to have people in our lives to love and supportive us in creating healthy environments in which to grow.

A good friend, John Bolinger, once shared with me, "When you are a child you love people because you need them. When you mature you need to have people around you that you love."

(Did you get that? If not, I'll wait. Go back and read it again.)

I had the privilege of working at Memorial Hospital in Chattanooga for seven years. When I think of support and encouragement, I think of someone very special at Memorial. Her name is Jessica Branch. Jessica is a wonderful person. She is everything you would ever imagine in a friend. She is kind, generous, thoughtful, considerate, and helpful. Everyone at Memorial loves her.

A few years ago, a house belonging to one of the employees burned down. Everything was destroyed. Jessie rallied everyone together and gathered money and clothes for the employee to start over.

Then, a few months later, I was having a rough week. I arrived at work and walked into my office. There on my desk was a vase of flowers. The attached note said, "Just thinking about you. Have a great day. Jessica Branch."

In seconds, my spirit was lifted from discouragement to encouragement. This little gift of thoughtfulness made my day!

The truth is Jessica Branch is not "someone" at Memorial Hospital, she is "everyone." She is an encouraging spirit that pervades the culture. Although Jessica is not real-life flesh and blood, she is alive and well. It is what makes Memorial Hospital the special place that it is.

When people come to work at Memorial, they are asked to be a Jessica. They are asked to look for opportunities to encourage others. An interesting phenomenon occurs when you encourage others: The more you encourage others, the more you are encouraged.

We all need connection. We all need support. We all need encouragement!

Being mutually supportive is 100% your choice! Shed or You're Dead*!

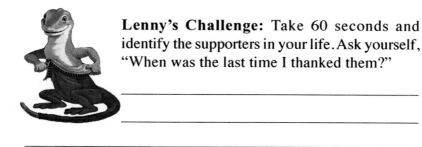

Lenny's Challenge: Take 60 seconds and identify the supporters in your life. Ask yourself, "When was the last time I thanked them?"

_____

_____

_____

_____

"The way to develop the best that is in a man
is by appreciation and encouragement."
Charles M. Schwab, Steel Tycoon

#22
CHEAT!

Yes, cheat! Go ahead, look over some else's shoulder and see if you can find the answers. And oh, your taxes? Come on, just fudge a little bit. Your chances of ever being caught are almost nil. Besides, I am sure the government owes it to you anyway. And your expense report, go ahead and add a few extra dollars, you have been working overtime, you deserve it!

Okay, Okay, Okay…maybe cheating is not the best idea. So, what can we learn from cheating?

The dictionary states that someone who cheats breaks the rules. They don't follow the conventional order. We all have grown up with rules. Our parents, our teachers, our bosses have all given us the list of "what to do," and "what not to do" in life.

As you continue to mature, it is helpful to stop and re-examine all those "must do's" and see if they still work for you. To look at throwing away the rules that no longer serve you or no longer make sense in your world. (CAUTION: I would suggest you be selective here and seriously consider which rules you should throw away. I tried to explain to the police why going 55 mph no longer served me well but all the officer did was SERVE ME a ticket!)

Some of the most successful people in history were those that challenged the rules.

A couple years ago, I was in Bentonville, Arkansas, presenting for Wal-Mart at their corporate offices. During my visit, I was amazed to hear about the history of the company and visit the first dime store where Sam Walton began.

The leading business experts of the day told Sam Walton that his strategy of placing huge Wal-Mart stores in small-town USA would never work. Well, as we all know, he proved them wrong and Wal-Mart became the largest retailer in the world. He broke the rules! They didn't work for him.

In fact, I saw the vehicle that Sam Walton drove until the time he died—an old red pickup truck. I am sure "the rules" say the richest man in America should be driving a luxury car. He broke the rules; again, they didn't work for him!

> **Breaking the rules (that no longer serve you) is 100% your choice! Shed or You're Dead°!**

Lenny's Challenge: Take 60 seconds and identify a rule you have been living with that doesn't work for you any more. Ask yourself, "Why doesn't it work?"

_____

_____

_____

_____

"It is good to obey all the rules when you're young, so you'll have the strength to break them when you're old."

Mark Twain, Great American Author

#23
BE A TYRANT!

Yes, be a tyrant. Be a dictator. Exercise your power in a harsh and cruel way. You are the ruler! You are in the one in power! Everyone else must bow to you!

Okay, Okay, Okay...becoming a "Little Hitler" may not work for very long. So, what can we possibly learn from the tyrant?

Tyrants have developed the skill of making rules and keeping them at all cost. They know the value of rules and how important order is in life. Not that any of us should aspire to become a dictator.

Now that I think about it...I do remember as a child my favorite bedtime story from the Bible was Moses coming to Pharaoh and saying, "Let my people go." Guess who I always wanted to be? Pharaoh! I would shout "NO, I will not let your people go!"

On the days that I was a "little less angelic" my mom took to calling me little Miss Pharaoh! I think it was mom's way of communicating to me that I had developed one of Pharaoh's skills quite well — stubbornness!

Anyway, the tyrant has mastered the ability of rule making. Why are rules important?

The accelerating rate of change necessitates equilibrium. How does change find the equilibrium? With order. All of us must have a certain degree of order and structure to be able to function. Our society needs order. That's why we have laws. If we didn't have them, we would have chaos.

Now you might be saying, "You're schizophrenic! You just said to break the rules, now you are telling me I need rules."

"YES!" But rules for your life that work for you, not ones that have been given to you and no longer serve a healthy purpose.

Several years ago, I developed my own rules. I prefer to call them guidelines for living. They are:

1. Eat healthy 80% of the time
2. Maintain my ideal weight
3. Exercise five days a week
4. Do one fun thing everyday
5. Journal daily and identifying a lesson learned and one thing I'm grateful for
6. Take off a minimum of two weeks a year
7. Read daily
8. Contribute 15% of my income to retirement
9. Contribute 10% of my income to savings
10. Encourage others (at least one person a day)
11. Meditate daily
12. Communicate assertively
13. Avoid negative people
14. Always strive to function outside my comfort zone
15. Give myself positive affirmations daily
16. Focus my energy on changing myself, not others
17. Communicate assertively
18. Give to others—time and money
19. Review my goals on a weekly basis
20. Filter everything I do in light of my personal mission:
    To love myself and to love others
    To grow myself and to help others grow
    To enjoy life and glorify God

The last few years have taught me that I function best when I follow my guidelines; I get myself in trouble when I don't.

**Developing your own life rules
is 100% your choice!
Shed or You're Dead*!**

Lenny's Challenge: Take 60 seconds (or more, you may need them here) and ask yourself, "What are my rules? My guidelines for living?"

_____

_____

_____

_____

_____

_____

_____

_____

_____

_____

_____

"When everything else fails, consider following the rules."
Anonymous

#24
PROCRASTINATE!

Yes, procrastinate! That report that is due, that house that needs cleaning, that job you are going to look for, that application to go back to school...don't worry about it. Why do today what you can put off until tomorrow? Besides, you are tired right now and you have LOTS of other things to do. Why don't you just veg out on the couch, watch TV and munch on some chips.

Okay, Okay, Okay...maybe putting things off is not the best way to live. I don't know...let me wait and think about it. So, what can we learn from procrastinating?

People who procrastinate are masters at postponing and delaying things. They have developed the ability to prioritize their needs. Now, some of us would argue with their prioritization, but they do make a conscious choice on which items to delay. They selectively do what they want to do and postpone everything else.

Might it be helpful to consider consciously postponing or delaying some things in our life? We all have multiple demands bombarding us everyday which, if not managed, can be overwhelming. Wouldn't it be helpful to sit down and list all the current life demands? Then, look at them to determine which ones I have to do now, which ones I can do later, and which ones I can just say NO to and not do at all!

Actually, prioritization is one of the healthiest coping skills to incorporate in your life. Tom Peters, management guru, credits one of his keys to success as his ability to identify and prioritize his top two things to do every day.

Prioritizing your life is 100% your choice!
Shed or You're Dead*!

Lenny's Challenge: Take 60 seconds and identify all your current demands. Ask yourself, "What do I have to do, what are other people asking me to do?" Now go back and write #1 by the ones that are top priority, #2 by the ones that are important and must be done soon, #3 by the ones that you need to delay for reevaluation at some later time in history, and draw a BIG FAT LINE through the ones that really don't need to do at all (or which you can delegate to someone else to do).

_____

_____

_____

_____

_____

_____

_____

_____

_____

_____

"Your success in life is largely determined
by your ability to say no."

Anonymous

#25
BE A COPYCAT!

Yes, be a copycat! Copy, copy, copy! You like the cool jacket your friend Edie has, go buy one. You like the new hairdo Carol has, go get one! You see that white Saab convertible that June has, go buy one! Don't be original, copy others, it's easier!

Okay, Okay, Okay…being someone's clone may not be the best idea. So, what can we learn from being a copycat?

Copycats have mastered the ability of taking on the characteristics and habits of others. And they do it quite well! If they see something they like, they copy it, they model it, they go buy it.

Might it not be helpful to learn from the copycat? You have to make sure you copycat the right people. Who do you admire? Who do you want to copy? Who is your role model? For me, I was fortunate to have an incredible role model as a mom.

Everyday, as I walked through the courtyard on the way to work at Memorial Hospital, I looked up to the third floor of the hospital. For just a second, a flashback of memories would flood my mind; some pleasant, but most of them not. I remember so many days and nights, so many holidays and birthdays celebrated here. Not by choice or because I worked here, but because my mom was dying of cancer.

Two years after battling the disease, in 1992, my mom died. During her last year alive, she kept a journal. It took five years after her death, but I finally mustered the courage to read it. As I opened her journal, I painfully read of her daily struggles, sometimes just to get out of bed. While going through chemotherapy and multiple surgeries, she suffered severe nausea and vomiting.

But during those trying days, one thing continually amazed me. Mom never looked at her circumstances and let them influence her attitude or how she was going to respond that day. Many days, after describing how bad she felt, Mom would end her journaling with "How can I be a blessing to someone today?"

So many times I distinctly recall friends leaving my mom's room and saying, "I came to encourage your mom, and I left feeling like she encouraged me."

I must admit, I have struggled with this. I don't understand the strength or courage that my mom was able to sustain. I can't comprehend how she did it.

My daily ritual of looking up to the third floor on the way into work is my way of bringing my life into perspective.

Some days, I have a tendency to complain when things don't go my way. Often times, I become negative when someone isn't as responsive as I would like. Frequently, I get upset and let petty issues drain my energy. But why? Why do I allow other people or circumstances control my attitude?

If my mom could have a great attitude and positive outlook on life in light of her situation, why can't I? If my mom could be happy lying in a hospital bed dying of cancer, why can't I?

Many days, I forget how much I have. I am healthy and have so much to be thankful for and I should be ecstatic as I walk into work everyday. I am not sure what my mom had, but I pray that whatever it is, I have it too.

Finding role models is 100% your choice!
Shed or You're Dead*!

 **Lenny's Challenge:** Take 60 seconds, and ask yourself, "Who do I want as a role model?" What do you admire about that person that you would like to copy?

_____

_____

_____

_____

"Ask counsel of him who governs himself well."
Leonardo da Vinci, Italian Artist

Lizard Factoid #5

An unhealthy lizard that is started on a healthy diet will often:

    A. Start shedding as normal but their skin will look darker.

    B. Not shed for a 2-3 months.

    C. Shed non-stop.

    D. Eat Healthy Choice Meals.

(Answer on next page)

Correct answer: C

If a reptile is unhealthy, it will not shed as often as it should. A formerly neglected and malnourished reptile that starts on a healthy diet and has a proper environment will often shed non-stop for several months as it undergoes a period of rapid growth.

Oh, so that explains it...

Whether you are a lizard or a human, if you want to shed and grow, it's important to establish healthy habits. Once you begin to create that healthy environment, you will be amazed how much you can grow.

**Establishing healthy habits
is 100% your choice!
Shed or You're Dead*!**

#26
BE A MISER!

Yes, be a miser! Don't spend any money. Especially on other people. Don't give back to anyone. Hoard! Don't contribute to anyone. Take it all in to yourself. Listen to what Benjamin told us, you know, "A penny saved is a penny earned." Then, after you save it, go bury it in the back yard. No, better yet, go stuff it in the mattress.

Okay, Okay, Okay…maybe hoarding money isn't the best strategy. So, what can we learn from the miser?

Misers have developed the skill of saving money. They are experts at it. Isn't it wise to save money? Especially in our day. Nothing can hamper shedding like being in survival mode. Most of us do not operate at our best from a state of panic.

Did you know that unemployment hit a record high of 15.27 million in 2010? You never know when something unexpectant will happen and you find yourself out of work. In the past, financial advisors would recommend keeping an emergency fund of three months living expenses in the bank. Today, many advisors are recommending you sock away at least eight months of living expenses.

Over twenty years ago, due to a marriage breakup, I was left financially destroyed. At 27 years of age, I ended up moving back in with my parents and took on three jobs until I dug my way out three years later. I made a commitment to myself that I would make it my practice to save 25% of my income, 10% for short term savings, and 15% for retirement.

I will admit, it was tough the first few years, but now I have adjusted my lifestyle to live below my means. Way below my means. Nothing can give more satisfaction than knowing that you have the ability and freedom to make more choices. It gives you the flexibility to give. Being strapped and living paycheck to paycheck can be limiting. Money is not evil, it is a tool that can allow for expanded choices in life.

Saving money is 100% your choice!
Shed or You're Dead*!

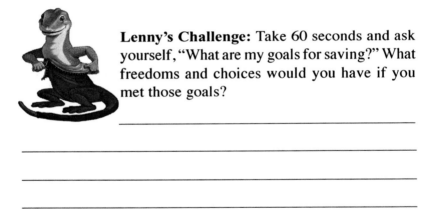

Lenny's Challenge: Take 60 seconds and ask yourself, "What are my goals for saving?" What freedoms and choices would you have if you met those goals?

_____

_____

_____

_____

"Never spend your money before you have it."
Thomas Jefferson, Founding Father

#27
BE A SNOB!

Yes, go ahead and be a snob! Don't talk to people, at least some people. Don't return those phone calls. Don't talk to the hired hands. Ignore them. They were only hired to do the work! Give them the cold shoulder. Sooner or later they will get the message. Remember, you are way above them. Disregard anyone who doesn't meet your standards. Keep your nose high!

Okay, Okay, Okay...seeing everyone else as socially inferior probably isn't the best way to live your life. So, what in the world can we learn from the snob?

Snobs have no problem deciding who they do and do not want to be around. They discriminate extremely well.

Is it right to discriminate? This world is filled with some very negative people. In fact, there are people in life whose mission it is to bring other people down. These people, if you allow them, will drain your energy and take you down with them. You know who I am talking about. Maybe it is a co-worker, a friend, a boss or even a spouse. No matter who it is, it ends the same. When you leave an interaction with these people, you just feel exhausted!

Wouldn't it be helpful to take a lesson from the snob and avoid negative people? Oh, none of us have the fortune of totally ridding them from our lives, but we can consciously decide to limit our expose to them to what is only absolutely necessary.

Avoiding negative people is 100% your choice!
Shed or You're Dead*!

Lenny's Challenge: Take 60 seconds and identify a person or a relationship that drains your energy? Write their initials here. _____

Ask yourself, "How can I limit my interactions with this person?"

_____

_____

_____

_____

"Avoid Negative People!"

Chinese Fortune Cookie

#28
BE THE CLASS CLOWN!

Yes, be the class clown. Goof off, make jokes. Don't work, don't study. Don't take life so seriously. Did you forget your whoopee cushion? What about your red sponge nose?

Okay, Okay, Okay…maybe wearing the red sponge nose is going a little too far. So, what can we possibly learn from the class clown?

The class clown is highly talented in one particular area. Laughter. Their focus is to find things in life that are funny, to laugh, and help other people laugh.

One of the healthiest coping mechanisms we can develop in life is to laugh. Laughter helps by:

- Boosting your immune system
- Relaxing your muscles
- Reducing your stress
- Reducing your blood pressure

Laughter just make us feel good!

I met a man recently who is starting opening up Laughter Clubs across the country. There are now over 450 clubs around the world. Many members claim that the Laughter Clubs have changed their entire outlook on life. In fact, 72% of Laughter Club members report improved interpersonal relations with co-workers, 85% say it has improved their self-confidence, and 66% suggest it has improved their ability to concentrate.

Now, you don't have to run out and necessarily join a laughter club, but incorporating laughter in your life is important. Here are a few ideas:

- Stop by a Hallmark store and take few minutes to read the funny cards.
- Find funny friends. Of all my friends, I have two or three who are hilariously funny. Not funny looking, but when I am around them, I laugh! I keep them on the top of my list and when I need a good laugh, I call them!
- Take a class. I have taken a couple, one on stand-up comedy and one on improv.
- Find a kid to play with you! The average child laughs 300-400 times a day versus 15 times a day for the average adult.

**Laughing is 100% your choice!
Shed or You're Dead*!**

Lenny's Challenge: Take 60 seconds and identify one thing you can do this week to incorporate laughter into your life (a movie, books, a night out with friends). Ask yourself, "What makes me laugh?"

_____

_____

_____

_____

"The most wasted of all days is one without laughter."
e.e. cummings, American Poet

#29
BE FICKLE!

Yes, be fickle! Change you mind, keep 'em guessing. Drive the waiter crazy! Order the filet mignon, Oh, no, you just saw what the lady next to you was eating. The pecan crusted salmon? It looks a lot better! No, you don't really want meat, ahh.... you're really in the mood for seafood! Waiter...

They say that it is a woman's prerogative to change her mind. Sorry men, we know we drive you crazy!

Okay, Okay, Okay...being fickle all the time would probably limit your ability to keep friends, dates, or jobs. So, what can we learn from being fickle?

Fickle people have developed the skill (and very adeptly I might add) of changing their mind. They are masters at it. If something isn't working, they change their mind. If something looks better, they change their mind. If the wind blows different, it must be a universal sign to change their mind.

Sometimes we can get stuck doing the same thing, the same way. It's like we beat ourselves over the head, we are bleeding and we keep banging. If something isn't working, might "being fickle" (changing our mind) sometimes help us with our approach.

This reminds me of Mary, one of my most memorable patients in the psychiatric unit.

"May I help you?" the muffled voice blared through the intercom system. I had just pushed the buzzer on the wall outside the psychiatric unit. "It's me, Kathy. Can you unlock the doors?" As the doors opened, I walked down the long hallway toward the nurse's station to go to my office. Stopping at the desk to get the morning report, I witnessed Mary, one of the patients, talking to Ken, the head nurse.

"Ken, unlock the doors, I need to go home," she demanded.

"I am sorry Mary, you can't go home. You need to go back to group and wait for your doctor to come." Ken responded.

Mary shook her head and said, "Okay," as she left the nurses station and slowly walked back into the group room.

A couple hours later, I saw Mary return again. She again demanded, "Ken, unlock the doors, I need to go home."

"I am sorry Mary, you can't go home. You need to go back to group and wait for your doctor to come." Ken responded once again.

Mary reacted like she did the first time. She shook her head and said, "Okay," and headed back to the group room.

An hour later, Mary returned yet another time. She looked up at Ken like it was the first time she had seen him all day and demanded for the third time, "Ken, unlock the doors, I need to go home."

What do you think Ken said? "Here are the keys!" (Just kidding!)

Although I am sure his frustration level has escalated to the point that he felt like opening the door and letting her go. With a stern but calm voice he responded, "I am sorry Mary, you can't go home. You need to go back to group and wait for your doctor to come."

What was Mary doing? She was doing the same thing over and over and expecting a different result.

Well, isn't that the definition of insanity? But don't we often do the same thing? And who was doing the same thing over and over? Mary? Ken? Or both?

If something isn't working, if you feel you are stuck, feel free to take a moment, be fickle and change your approach!

**Changing your approach is 100% your choice!
Shed or You're Dead™!**

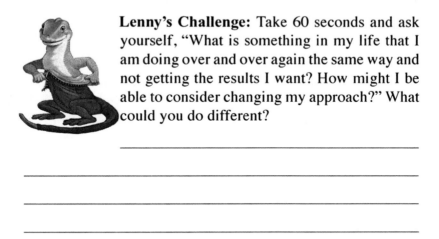

Lenny's Challenge: Take 60 seconds and ask yourself, "What is something in my life that I am doing over and over again the same way and not getting the results I want? How might I be able to consider changing my approach?" What could you do different?

_____

_____

_____

_____

"Insanity is doing the same thing, the same way,
and expecting a different result."
Albert Einstein, Physicist

#30
BE A CONTROL FREAK!

Yes, be a control freak! Take control...of EVERYTHING! You can do it. Don't allow others to say, to think, or to do. You tell them! You know you can do it better, faster, quicker, cheaper. By the way, where are your remote controls? You sleep with them in your hand, don't you?

Okay, Okay, Okay...So setting your life's goal to be king and keeper of the remote is probably not the best idea. So, what can we learn from the control freak?

Control freaks have an obsession to exert control over their environment. They want to control what others say, do, and even THINK! Now, this may be challenging for a few of you to answer, but what skill do you think the control freaks have developed? CONTROL!

Wouldn't it be helpful to realize that each one of us has 100% control? Not over every situation, but we have 100% control over our responses. No one can take that away from us. The tragedy is that most of us don't acknowledge that we're internally equipped with that kind of power. Often we fall victim to circumstances.

In 1977, George Valliant wrote a book called *Adaptation to Life*. It was a long-term study of the brightest of the bright. The research took a 40 year look at 100 men's lives from Harvard University. As they grew up, the study continued to follow their lives. What happened to them? How did they respond?

What they found was remarkable. Some of the men had traumatic events of death, divorce and financial troubles inflict their lives. Yet upon interviewing them year after year, they were functioning well. On the other hand, some of the men in the study had what most of us would consider very few stressors in life. Oddly enough, upon interviewing them, they found mental illness, sickness, dysfunctional relationships and suicide. The study suggests that it is not the events that happen to us, but how we respond or cope to the events that matters.

The final conclusion is that we all use coping mechanisms to deal with life. The degree to which we are successful and happy is the degree to which we develop and use healthy and mature coping mechanisms.

Here are the five healthiest coping strategies discussed from the study.

1. Humor – Laughter. We know this. But often times we just laugh this one away. We don't recognize how healthy it is for us. Research tells us that when we laugh we release endorphins into our body that help us deal with stress.

2. Altruism – Help someone else. Guess what, it works! One day while sitting as the administrator of psychiatric services for the hospital, I had one of those days from Hell. Budget issues, staff issues, why am I here issues. I tossed my papers up on my desk and grabbed my guitar and walked out on the psychiatric unit to spend some time talking and singing with the patients. It was the healthiest things I could have done. (Little did I realize at the time that the psychiatric patients were the sanest bunch of people I had dealt with all day.)

3. Sublimation – Channeling the negative energy into a positive path, one that is socially acceptable. You might be furious with your spouse for not remembering your birthday but instead of exploding, you decide to channel the anger by going for a walk or riding your bike.

4. Anticipation – Future planning for unexpected events. You know your mother is going to die soon so you begin the anticipatory grieving process. Mentally, you begin to plan for the future discomfort. "Expect for the best, plan for the worst."

5. Suppression – Prioritizing. You are not in denial. You are not repressing. You acknowledge all the demands on you and decide you can only do so much. Most of you probably remember watching the final scene in *Gone with the Wind*. Scarlett O'Hara says, "Tomorrow is another day." We are living in a world that is bombarding us with more and more demands everyday. It is not humanly possible to do them all. The key is to identifying your demands, then deciding which one need to be done today, or tomorrow or maybe don't even need to be done at all.

> **Exercising control of yourself is
> 100% your choice!
> Shed or You're Dead*!**

 **Lenny's Challenge:** Take 60 seconds and ask yourself, "What are two healthier ways I can take control over my responses?"

_____

_____

"Happiness is about 10% what happens to you
and 90% how you respond."

Charles Swindoll, Author

#31
LIMIT YOUR VOCABULARY!

Yes, I said limit your vocabulary! Learning new words isn't important. After all, you are not competing in any spelling bee. Multi-syllabic words are tough to remember and will clog your head with words that are hard to pronounce! Don't worry about it; many people don't even know what they mean. Who wants to win at Scrabble anyway!

Okay, Okay, Okay…maybe scoring 72 points by spelling "MILK" on a triple word square isn't so bad. So, what can we learn from limiting our vocabulary?

No matter how large our vocabulary is, we tend to repeat certain key words over and over again. Words are very powerful. In seconds, they have the capacity to catapult you to the top of the world or plunge you to the depths of despair. Just think about it. How do you feel when someone says, "You are awesome!" vs. "You screwed up?"

It is one challenge to master a large vocabulary; it's another to master a vocabulary of a few choice words and to use them wisely. If you did, what might the few choice words be?

"Thanks."
"I'm grateful."
"I love you."
"You're special."

These all come to mind.

Words also help us to appreciate our own situation and that of others.

Several years ago, I moved up north and experienced plenty of snow challenges. Planning on a stress-free two hour flight down south to speak at a conference, blizzard storms moved in and I never made it to "82 degree sunny Miami, Florida!"

Stuck at an airport after seven (!) cancelled flights, I heard lots of yelling and screaming and complaining. After several days of inconvenience and lost income, I became upset.

Finally, they shut the airport down. On the way to the hotel to sleep over for the night, I struck up a conversation with a teenage boy traveling alone seated beside me. "Where were you trying to go?" I asked. "Atlanta," the young man replied, "to my father's funeral." In a calm voice he continued, "It looks like I am not going to make it."

REALITY CHECK! Immediately, my week of inconveniences didn't seem so important any longer. I had thought I had it bad. I was quickly reminded of someone who had it much worse.

After I settled in my hotel room for the night, I took the opportunity that the young man no longer had with his father. I grabbed the phone and called a dear friend. The first thing out of my mouth was, "Thanks for being in my life. You are an awesome friend. I love you."

We never know what a day will bring forth. Don't wait to use a few choice words wisely! Say the words now!

**Using words wisely is 100% your choice!
Shed or You're Dead*!**

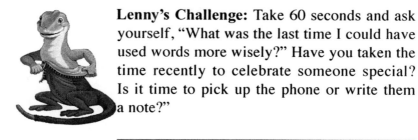 **Lenny's Challenge:** Take 60 seconds and ask yourself, "What was the last time I could have used words more wisely?" Have you taken the time recently to celebrate someone special? Is it time to pick up the phone or write them a note?"

_____

_____

_____

_____

"Handle them carefully, for words have
more power than atom bombs."

Pearl Strachan Hurd, Wise Woman

Lizard Factoid #6

Within the Native American Tradition, lizards represent:

A. Dreams.

B. A holy aspect of the animal world.

C. Good luck.

D. The Friday night special at the local Indian bar and grill.

(Answer on next page)

Correct Answer: A

Lizards are often depicted by the Native Indian culture as dreams, the shadow side of reality.

So that explains it...

For us humans, dreams are where reality begins. For if we can dream it, believe it, and act on it, all things are possible. Throughout the world of dreams, all levels of awareness are accessible.

What are your dreams? What do you want to shed? What do you want to look like in your new skin?

After reading this book, I trust that you will make a conscious decision to embrace life-long growth. My hope is that from now on, whenever you see a lizard, it will serve as a mental trigger and remind you to keep shedding.

**Making dreams a reality is
100% your choice!
Shed or You're Dead*!**

Lenny Speaks

"Kathy, don't you just love her? Uses lots of words to say stuff. Here is my take on the unconventional strategies."

Habits that Harm	Habits that Help
Be Psychotic	Listen to Your Inner Voice
Be Emotional	Live Your Passion
Hallucinate	Visualize
Be Blunt	Be Honest
Be Obsessive	Focus
Be a Cry Baby	Grieve Losses
Be Pessimistic	Plan for the Worst
Be a Pollyanna	Expect the Best
Brown Nose	Build Self-Esteem
Don't Wear Clean Underwear	Don't Worry
Be a Know-It-All	Be a Life-Long Learner
Lose Your Memory	Live in the Present
Eat Two Crickets a Day	Nurture Yourself Daily
Make Mistakes	Learn from Your Failures

Habits that Harm	Habits that Help
Don't Conserve	Utilize Your Resources
Get Angry	Express Feelings Appropriately
Bug People	Ask Questions, Get the Facts
Be Narcissistic	Take Care of Yourself
Be Impulsive	Make Decisions
Act Childish	Be Yourself
Be Codependent	Be Mutually Supportive
Cheat	Break the Rules
Be a Tyrant	Develop Your Own Rules
Procrastinate	Prioritize
Be a Copycat	Find Role Models
Be a Miser	Save Money
Be a Snob	Avoid Negative People
Be the Class Clown	Laugh
Be Fickle	Change Your Approach
Be a Control Freak	Exercise 100% Control of Yourself
Limit Your Vocabulary	Use Words Wisely

Sometimes bad habits get in the way of shedding. With my laser lizard focus, I dug deep until I found the morsel of truth in each of the habits that hurt. And in that search, I discovered the habits that help me shed my skin.

What Happens if You Decide Not to Shed?

"The tragedy of man is what dies
inside of himself while he still lives."

Albert Schweitzer, Theologian

It happened like clockwork. Friday night at 10 p.m. The Emergency Room doors flew open and in rolled Medic 5. The squeaky wheels of the stretcher stopped abruptly at my triage desk. "Where should I put him?" Paramedic Stone announced as he handed me the ambulance report. "Just put him on the stretcher in the hallway," I abruptly responded.

It was George. It was the same song and dance every Friday night. George was a disheveled 46 year old man. His bloodshot eyes bulged from the cheap wine he consumed. His oily matted hair stained the ER sheets. His breath reeked of rotten eggs and his tattered denim shirt only got dirtier as the weeks went by.

For the past four years he had qualified for the ER frequent flyer program. Every week he would come in intoxicated, then he'd lie in the hallway until he sobered up enough for the police to take him to jail. Week after week the frustration swelled as I continued to help a man who, for some reason, wasn't helping himself.

One Friday night, the ER doors flew opened as they typically did but this time something was different. It was George — but today he walked in. I was in shock! Slowly George approached my Triage Desk and sat down. Feeling a bit awkward, I began taking his vital signs. Although I knew George well, I had never had a face to face conversation with him while he was sober.

As I took the blood pressure cuff of his arm, I thought to myself, I have to know. I must ask. Interested to discover how he had come to this abysmal state in life, I mustered the courage and said "George, you have been coming in here every week drunk for years. It's the same story every time. You lie on the stretcher till you sober up enough to be hulled off to jail. Help me understand WHY?"

He paused for a second, and then he took a deep breath, then with his voice trembling, he slowly looked up to me and his eyes began to water.

"I know you might find this hard to believe, but I was a very successful businessman in this town. Several years ago my wife and two children were driving home and a car went out of control and hit them head on. Instantaneously, they all died."

"I couldn't handle the pain. I couldn't deal with it. I started drinking to cope. The drinking got so bad that I eventually lost my job, then my house, then I ended up on the streets." As tears streamed down his face, he said "I DIED TOO!"

My heart sank. What a travesty. George was right. Although he was not in the car the night of the accident, he did die too. Oh, not physically (although his drinking was damaging his body) but emotionally, mentally, socially, financially, and spiritually, George was dead.

Through this tragic event, he had become stuck. He had been unable to shed. Although my heart went out to him, for some reason he had made a choice not to get help.

I never saw George after that day. I often wondered what

happened to him. Is he still alive? Did he continue to drink? Did he die underneath a bridge somewhere?

Was that day the beginning of his road to recovery?

And for our final so what? So, what can we possibly learn from a drunk?

I will let you determine this one for yourself. I can tell you what I learned. Of all the people I have had the fortune of meeting in my life, George has been my greatest teacher, my greatest motivator.

That brief interaction with George was one of the most powerful five minutes of my life. I realized that life is full of losses. I couldn't avoid it. I realized that life was short. I couldn't escape it. I realized that people get stuck. I wasn't helping them get unstuck. I realized that up until this point in my life I was putting a Band-Aid on people's physical needs.

But so often their true wounds are emotional and all the first aid in the world won't help. Until those issues were addressed, they would continue to come through the revolving ER door.

The next day, I quit my job as an ER nurse and decided to go back to graduate school to get a degree in counseling. I found a job as a nurse working at a psychiatric hospital with troubled teenagers. I committed to helping people with not only their physical needs but also their emotional ones.

I also realized the costly price of not shedding. What happens if you don't move past the loss? If you focus on the loss and get stuck long enough it will eventually destroy you.

Most of us probably won't experience the tragic loss of our entire family at once like George did, but who is to say how our lives will unfold. We can't predict it, we can't control it. All we can do is commit to the notion that no matter what life hands us that we will make the choice to shed. And if we get stuck, we will get help.

My hope is that George will somehow motivate you also. If you have a job you hate, quit it. If you are in an unhealthy relationship, leave it. If you have a passion, a vision of what you want to be in life, do it!

One Final Thought

As you shed, focus on the gains, not the losses.

Now that's easier said than done, right? Yes, focusing on what you have, not what you don't have is not easy. I must admit, sometimes I have a tendency to throw a "poor-pitiful me" party. Guess who I invite to the party? Yes, all my "losses" and "don't haves," and "wish I would haves," not to mention my "been throughs!"

I've lost my mom, I've lost my dad, I've been divorced, I've been financially destroyed, I've had cancer, I've been through an AIDS crisis, I've lost a dream job, I've had various health problems, I've had multiple surgeries, I've lost my ability to have children, I've moved to a new city, I've lost the relationship I moved for and the future dreams that went with it, I've lost my local established friends, I've no place to call home. It can go on and on…

I have discovered that life puts "shoulds" on us. We are told from the time we are a kid about how we should have a "normal" life, a "secure" job, a "life-long" spouse, 2.5 "perfect" kids, a freshly painted white picket fence…and the outcome is…you will live happily ever after.

Guess what? That's a fairy tale!! If you measure life with the "should" ruler you will always come up short! The sooner you SHED that myth the happier you will be.

My losses have provided me the opportunity to shed

probably more than the average person (and let me just say I have a TONS more to shed!) But with each shed comes the opportunity to grow, to learn, to develop new relationships and to see life in a different way.

Peace only comes when you let go and realize it's all part of life. That just as the seasons pass, so does the cycle of shedding and the detachment of the old and the new attachment to the new. With each new attachment comes the gains.

You have heard about my losses, did you hear about my gains? Do you want to know what my new skin looks like?

I've developed new friendships, created deeper and more significant relationships, adopted new family members (really cool!), developed new financial skills, grew up, became more independent and became a great AUNT. I've found my inner strength, realized I am more than a role or title in life, started to appreciate more of every moment of life, helped more people, found my passion, learned from new experiences, and made sure I was grateful at the end of each day for what I had.

Let me encourage you to go back and read my acknowledgment page, I have been blessed with some incredible friends, many of which I consider part of my adopted family. Let me take this opportunity to thank them again.

Thank You!

But why in the world would I ever think differently? Mom said it would be that way!

Life is all about choices.

Shed or You're Dead®.

And I am not dead!

Ready - Set - Shed:
Successful Shedding for You!

Complete the following sentences to help you further explore how you can shed.

1. What I am most passionate about is…

2. What creates energy for me is…

3. My life would be more filling if…

4. I have the most difficulty shedding…

5. I feel I could make significant leaps if I only would …

6. I am happiest when…

7. When I am 80 years old, the three things I want people to say about me are…

8. I am most proud of my ability to...

9. What I look like in my new skin is...(Describe who you want to be)

10. If I had the courage, I would...

11. What is holding me back from this is....

12. My strengths are...

13. My opportunities for growth are...

14. The people who can help mentor and guide me are...

15. The three things I can do this week to move me closer to my goals are...

16. The two crickets that I need to eat (do) everyday to continue to shed are...

17. My greatest fear is...

Shredding Exercise

You have three choices.

    1 Use this page and tear it out of the book.

    2. Use this page and photocopy it.

    3. Get a blank sheet of paper as a worksheet.

Yea, go ahead, you really have to do this.

Write down the most memorable mistakes you have made, all the faults that you have. All the things you think you should have done in your life...

_____

_____

_____

_____

_____

_____

_____

_____

_____

_____

_____

_____

Now, if you choose #1 and used this page, tear it out of the book. If you choose #2 or #3, grab your sheet of paper in your hand. This is a three step process.

1. Rip the paper in half.

2. Rip it in half again.

3. Continue ripping until you can hardly see the pieces of paper. (151 different pieces if you want to be exact.) Go for it. SHRED and SHED!

Let it go…shed the past. Forgive yourself from all the faults and mistakes you think you made. The past is the past. Your shedding future is now here!

"As long as you don't forgive, who and whatever it is
will occupy rent-free space in your mind."
Isabelle Holland, Author

MY PERSONAL SHEDDING PLAN

Now that you have completed the book, we have come to the most important part. What does shedding mean to you? What are you going to do different tomorrow as a result?

Lenny's Challenge: Take a moment and flip back through the book. Star the three most significant strategies to you.

Habits that Harm	Habits that Help
Be Psychotic	Listen to Your Inner Voice
Be Emotional	Live Your Passion
Hallucinate	Visualize
Be Blunt	Be Honest
Be Obsessive	Focus
Be a Cry Baby	Grieve Losses
Be Pessimistic	Plan for the Worst
Be a Pollyanna	Expect the Best
Brown Nose	Build Self-Esteem

Habits that Harm	Habits that Help
Don't Wear Clean Underwear	Don't Worry
Be a Know-It-All	Be a Life-Long Learner
Lose Your Memory	Live in the Present
Eat Two Crickets a Day	Nurture Yourself Daily
Make Mistakes	Learn from Your Failures
Don't Conserve	Utilize Your Resources
Get Angry	Express Feelings Appropriately
Bug People	Ask Questions, Get the Facts
Be Narcissistic	Take Care of Yourself
Be Impulsive	Make Decisions
Act Childish	Be Yourself
Be Codependent	Be Mutually Supportive
Cheat	Break the Rules
Be a Tyrant	Develop Your Own Rules
Procrastinate	Prioritize
Be a Copycat	Find Role Models
Be a Miser	Save Money
Be a Snob	Avoid Negative People
Be the Class Clown	Laugh
Be Fickle	Change Your Approach
Be a Control Freak	Exercise 100% Control of Yourself
Limit Your Vocabulary	Use Words Wisely

What are three key ideas out of all the ones you jotted down.

1. _____

_____

_____

_____

2. _____

_____

_____

_____

3. _____

_____

_____

_____

Now identify below what are you going to START doing, what are you going to STOP doing, what are you going to CONTINUE doing from this day forth. (I hope you have been validated and recognize you are doing some things very well).

Note: The more measurable, specific and time limited, the more likely that you will follow through. (Example—I am going to start eating two crickets a day, nurturing myself daily, by going to the gym 5 days a week and exercising for 30 minutes and meditating every morning for 20 minutes.

START

STOP

CONTINUE

ABOUT
KATHY B. DEMPSEY

Best known for her creative, unique and innovative approach, Kathy's presentations are engaging, highly interactive and packed full of content for immediate implementation.

Kathy is President of Keep Shedding! Inc., a company that ignites organizations with the practical skills and motivation to lead and master change.

Her most popular book, Shed or You're Dead®: 31 Unconventional Strategies for Change and Growth is the recipient of a Writer's Digest International Book Award.

Kathy is also a contributing author for two of the bestselling Chicken Soup for the Soul series. Her most recent publications are the popular Shed or You're Dead Survival Guides.

Kathy led Memorial Health Care System's organizational development efforts to become one of the top 100 hospitals in America.

The Georgia Speakers Association voted Kathy as the Showcase Speaker of the Year and its Master of Influence Honoree. Bob Pike's Creative Training Techniques International also named her the Trainer of the Year. Kathy is the Past

President of the National Speakers Association, Philadelphia Chapter.

She has achieved the highest earned speaker's designation in the world, the Certified Speaking Professional (CSP).

A few of Kathy's clients/sponsors include: American Express, Johnson & Johnson, Disney, John Hopkins, Procter & Gamble, SHRM, Walmart, Delta Air Lines, GSK, Honeywell, Wells Fargo and Verizon Wireless.

Kathy received her Master's of Education in Psychology from the University of Tennessee. A native of Washington D.C, Kathy now resides in Scottsdale, Arizona.

Kathy B. Dempsey

Kathy@KeepShedding.com

www.KeepShedding.com

NEED SUPPORT
TO HELP YOU SHED?

Sign up for 60 Seconds of Shedding from Lenny the Lizard, a quick monthly ezine, to help you with just 60 seconds of counsel to assist you as you shed old habits and thinking and enable personal, professional and organizational growth.

The decision to shed is hard, but it only takes a second. Continuing to shed takes commitment, perseverance and the encouragement and support of others.

Sign up by visiting www.KeepShedding.com or sending an email to Lenny@KeepShedding.com and write "subscribe" in the subject line.

CPSIA information can be obtained at www.ICGtesting.com
Printed in the USA
BVOW020139200911

271609BV00005B/1/P

9 780974 292625